The Money Management Game

The Money Management Game

What They Don't Tell You About Mutual Funds

by
Andy Filipiuk

General Editors:
Mark Filipiuk, B.Com., LL.B, J.D.
Marc Jennings, M.A.

Produced and packaged by:
Burgher Books
555 Richmond Street West
Toronto, Ontario
M5V 3B1

Cover design by Ink Design Communications

Canadian Cataloguing in Publication Data

Filipiuk, Andy
    The money management game

Includes Bibliographical references and index.
ISBN 0-9682661-0-X

1. Mutual funds.
I. Filipiuk Investment Corporation   II. Title

HG4530.F485 1997   332.63 ' 27   C97-931785-1

Distributed by:
Hushion House
36 Northline Road
Toronto, Ontario
M4B 3E2 Canada

Printed and bound in Canada

97 98 99 00   5 4 3 2 1

Acknowledgements

I would like to thank the following individuals for their help and for the contributions they made to the book. Marc Jennings and Mark Filipiuk, for their superb editorial work in putting the whole project together. Bill Filipiuk, for his work on the Stromberg Report and his research contributions. David Lepoidevin, my former desk partner, and currently a Vice-President of a major Canadian brokerage house in Vancouver, for his contributions and recommendations, and his remarkable knowledge of the mutual fund and brokerage industry. Thanks to Marion Filipiuk, Paul Filipiuk, Chris Laframboise, Jim Cole, Prof. Jack Winder, Bill Robson of the C.D. Howe Institute, and my staff, Jim Kay et al., for their time and effort in helping free up my time for this endeavour. And a special thanks to all the proofreaders of the original draft, for the time they dedicated, and all the helpful recommendations they made.

Table of Contents

Table of Contents

Chapter 5– Who Sells Equity Mutual Funds and How Are They Regulated?

Chapter 6– Understanding Prospectuses and Mutual Fund Investment Styles

Table of Contents

Chapter 7– Mutual Fund Sales Charges and Fees

Chapter 8– How Taxes and Inflation Affect Your Mutual Fund Returns

Chapter 9– Evaluating Equity Mutual Fund Performance

Chapter 10 – Long Term Track Records for Equity Mutual Funds

Chapter 11 – Comparing Equity Mutual Funds to Other Asset Classes

Chapter 12 – Should You Buy Bonds Yourself, or Invest in Bond Mutual Funds?

Chapter 13 – Tricks of the Trade

Chapter 14 – RRSPs: Changing Policies and Foreign Content

Chapter 15 – Index Funds, Hedge Funds, Funds of Funds and Derivatives

Chapter 16 – Recommendations

Table of Contents

Introduction

Since the beginning of this decade, the mutual fund industry has grown at a staggering rate. There are currently over 7000 mutual funds available to purchasers in the United States and over 70 million mutual fund accounts. In Canada, the amount of money invested in all fund groups has risen from $20 billion in 1990 to over $258 billion by June of 1997. In other words, over 90% of the money in mutual funds in Canada at present has been invested since 1990. During this time the North American equity and bond markets have performed extremely well. So well, in fact, that by most traditional yardsticks for measuring stock values, they are at all-time highs.

You can't help but notice all the articles about mutual funds in the media, the tremendous amount of advertising the fund companies are doing to bring in more money and the growing number of industry participants in this field. The money management game is a very high margin business. During a strong bull market the amount of money to be made is gigantic. The Canadian banks and trust companies have become ever more focused on increasing the amount of managed money under administration and have significantly increased their product lines. Even bank tellers are being licensed to help sell the in-house products.

The equity markets as measured by the major indexes have averaged a little over a 10% compounded rate of return over the past 50 years. But how well have equity mutual funds as a whole done? There is no ready answer to this question, but it is quite realistic to assume that most fundholders have come nowhere close to those market index rates of return.

With all the money that has gone into mutual funds in the past six years, one of the burning questions is how much of this new money is "hot," or speculative, and what percentage is really invested for the long term. Peter Lynch, the former manager of the world's largest mutual fund, Fidelity Magellan, commented on one of the nightly business programs that, despite his 29% compounded rate of return over a 10-year period, 50% of the fund's shareholders had lost money. While Fidelity later denied Lynch's statement, his point was well taken. Investors often get in and out of funds at the wrong time.

An even more pressing question is how much the investing public really knows about mutual funds. Filtering through all of the information with which we're bombarded is next to impossible. How do we evaluate performance records (which in many instances can be a little misleading), understand the level of risk involved, and actually choose funds that suit our needs, when most mutual fund prospectuses are written in a language that is foreign to most of us?

The purpose of this book is straightforward: to show the reader how the managed money and/or mutual fund industry operates, from how to understand a mutual fund prospectus, and what type of fees one can expect to pay, to who gets paid (including how much and how often), and what rate of return an investor can realistically expect. An attempt will be made to describe all the mutual fund products currently available, the different ways of buying them, and how they compare with other non-managed money products. No investment advice will be given with respect to the products discussed, but various mutual fund investment strategies will be presented.

The book is divided into 16 chapters, each with a list of main topics at the beginning and a summary of key points at the end, so that easy reference can be made for specific questions that the reader may want to answer quickly. To illustrate the points being made, I have added many anecdotal passages drawn from my experience of working in the financial services industry.

I truly hope that you will gain from this book a greater knowledge of the inner workings of the mutual fund industry so that you can enjoy the benefits of asset appreciation and avoid the potential pitfalls along the way.

Andy Filipiuk, September 1997

Chapter 1

What Are Mutual Funds?

A mutual fund is a pool of money to which investors contribute. Depending on how much money each investor puts in, he or she is allotted a certain number of shares or "units" in the fund. This pool of money is invested by a professional money manager (professional in the sense that the money manager is being paid by the investors), who must be licensed by the securities regulator. The money may be invested in a number of different kinds of investments, which are guided by the stated objectives of the fund's prospectus. Mutual funds are *not* insured by the Canada Deposit Insurance Corporation and no guarantees with regard to performance are made, with the possible exception of segregated funds offered by insurance companies. The assets within a fund are administered by a trustee, so if the fund manager or fund company goes bankrupt or goes out of business, the assets of the fundholders are safely held by a third party (the trustee). Fund buyers often have little understanding of this aspect of mutual funds.

There are three main types of mutual funds. They are differentiated by the kinds of assets in which each type of mutual fund invests:

- **Money market funds** invest in debt instruments with durations of 90 days or less,

- **Bond funds** invest in debt instruments of durations which generally range from 1 to 30 years (although some extend as far as 100 years) and

- **Equity funds** invest in shares (or ownership) of publicly traded companies.

In This Chapter:

- **Open-end Funds**

- **Closed-end Funds**

- **What Do Mutual Funds Invest In?**

- **Money Market Funds**

- **Bond Funds**

- **Equity Funds**

- **Key Points**

In addition to being differentiated by the kinds of assets in which they invest, mutual funds may also be categorized as either open-end or closed-end funds.

Open-end Funds

Open-end mutual funds have an unlimited number of units (or shares) available. Every time a new investor buys into these funds, more units are created. The price of these units is determined by the total value of the assets (net of liabilities) divided by the number of shares outstanding at the end of each day (some funds are valued weekly and some monthly). Open-end mutual funds are far more common than the closed-end variety (99% of all mutual fund assets are open-end) and their prices are printed daily in most newspapers. The investor can place buy and sell orders through his or her broker (or licensed salesperson), or place orders directly through the fund company or institution where the assets are held.

Closed-end Funds

Closed-end mutual funds issue a fixed number of shares and trade on a stock exchange. A buyer can buy the closed-end fund upon its initial issue (or creation) or buy it after it has been traded on a stock exchange.

Each of the two types of funds mentioned above has certain advantages and disadvantages. Open-end funds are valued daily so that the investor knows what the price will be if he or she decides to sell. The selling price, however, is set at the end of the day, or after the markets close. In other words, the price may change during the day, so that only a rough estimate of the selling price is possible. The manager must ensure that there is enough cash on hand to pay out the redemptions in case a lot of sell orders are received. If there is not enough cash on hand, stocks or bonds in the portfolio may have to be sold to raise the cash for the redemption orders, which may have to be done at an unfavourable time (when the value of the asset holdings is down).

It is worth noting that there are currently mutual funds in the U.S. that have a negative cash position. Some of these funds have borrowed against the value of the fund in order to buy more stock (effectively leveraging the fund). This is a very dangerous practice that could snowball if the stock prices drop and redemption orders start to come in quickly. Normally, instead of leveraging, most open-end funds have a provision by which they can borrow money (up to 5% of the fund's assets) to help pay out cash when a large number of redemption orders come in, so that they can prevent a disorderly selling of stock from within the fund. This is a safety measure to help protect the fundholders' capital in tumultuous times, which is quite different from borrowing money for leverage purposes. Fundholders should be aware that leveraging may occur from time to time in some non-Canadian funds (the practice is not permitted in Canada). Where it is permitted, the practice is rare and must be declared in the particular fund's prospectus.

Managers of closed-end funds don't have to worry about having to sell the portfolio holdings at unfavourable prices. Because the manager is given a fixed amount of money upon issue, he or she can exercise full control over the management of that pool of money. The fundholders, when they wish to sell, must sell in the market instead of doing a redemption, and market prices may be at a discount from the net asset value of the fund at the time. For example, the intrinsic value of a given fund's units may be $10 (which represents the market value of the fund's assets divided by the number of shares) although the fund may only actually be trading at $9.75 on the stock exchange. Conversely, a fund with a net asset value of $10 could actually trade at a premium, e.g. at $10.25, on the stock exchange. The price of closed-end funds is determined by market sentiment: whether investors are optimistic or pessimistic about the future prospects of the fund's holdings. Investors who buy closed-end funds can often do very well by purchasing these funds at a discount and either patiently waiting for the market sentiment to improve or simply letting the assets within the fund appreciate.

It is possible for a closed-end fund to be changed to an open-end fund. This situation will usually arise when a closed-end fund has continually traded at a discount for a long period of time. The fund manager or shareholders may wish to vote to change the fund to an open-ended one, thus allowing the fundholders to cash in or sell their units at the real asset price of the fund (if they wish to do so). This scenario has been played out by various funds listed on the Toronto Stock Exchange (TSE) in recent years. Of course, the investor who buys a fund at a discount shortly before the particular fund changes to an open-ended one, stands to benefit substantially from the well-timed purchase!

In addition to the above scenario, some closed-end funds have recently been created with a closing date, i.e., a date on which the fund will officially end. This special feature ensures that the initial investors will eventually get access to their money at net asset value. Setting a closing date is an attempt to prevent these funds from trading at too great a discount. The gap between the fund's discount price and its net asset value should narrow as the fund's closing date approaches.

Finally, many closed-end funds have lower management fees because there are no ongoing advertising, marketing or distribution costs and thus many of the operating expenses are lower.

What Do Mutual Funds Invest In?

There are currently over 1500 mutual funds available to Canadian investors. The growth in the number of funds in 1996 was 40%. This amazing statistic shows the magnitude of the recent popularity of these investments. It also raises some interesting questions that will be discussed later in this book.

Money Market Funds

These funds generally invest in treasury bills, bankers acceptances (promissory notes issued by corporations and guaranteed by banks), and corporate paper (short-term promissory notes issued by major corporations) of a duration of 90 days or less. Money market funds are, in most instances, a holding tank for cash. They are usually used in the short term by investors who are either waiting to buy an asset, or who have just sold one. The long-term benefits of keeping cash in this type of fund are minimal (or quite possibly non-existent when taxes and inflation are considered).

Money market funds offer investors good liquidity. Generally, small investors can get a better rate of return on shorter-term interest rates by investing in money market funds than by keeping their money in banks or investing in short-term debt instruments themselves. (Funds can invest in large quantities of debt instruments and can get institutional pricing.)

Bond Funds

These funds generally invest in government debt (federal, provincial and municipal), as well as corporate bonds with maturities that can extend up to 30 years (and as far as 100 years). The money manager's objective is to maximize the income return as well as to potentially achieve some capital gains (when interest rates decline — see Chapter 12). Bond funds will generally outperform money market funds over time. They will also outperform equities over certain time periods as well. Because bond funds are able to take positions in longer bond maturities, they can offer greater income than money markets (the longer the term of the bond, the greater the risk and, as a result, the greater the interest rate received in most cases). Bond funds do, however, have greater risk than money market funds, as it is possible to lose capital in a bond fund when interest rates rise. The longer the bond fundholder remains in the fund, the greater the chance that any such loss will turn into a gain.

Equity Funds

These funds are designed to invest in the common shares of companies. In other words, they assume an ownership position in businesses that will primarily provide capital gains and dividend income to their investors.

Besides the three above-mentioned classes of funds, there is a great deal of variation in the kinds of investments that can constitute the asset make-up of any particular fund. Some of the more popular investments are:

- Money Market — Canadian and U.S. Funds

- Bond Funds — Domestic and Foreign, Mortgage Funds and Dividend Funds

- Equity Funds — Canadian (RRSP Eligible), U.S. and International Equity (RRSP-eligible as foreign content)

- Specialty Funds — Precious Metals, Short Funds, Emerging Market Funds

- Sector Funds — e.g. High-Tech, Real Estate

- Balanced Funds — Mutual funds holding a combination of cash, bonds and stocks

- Income Trust Units — Oil and Gas and Real Estate (REITs are governed by trust agreement, although they are very similar to mutual funds)

- Hedge Funds, Index Funds and Funds of Funds

- Labour-Sponsored Funds and Venture Capital Funds

The graph below shows where each type of mutual fund or trust may lie along the risk/reward continuum.

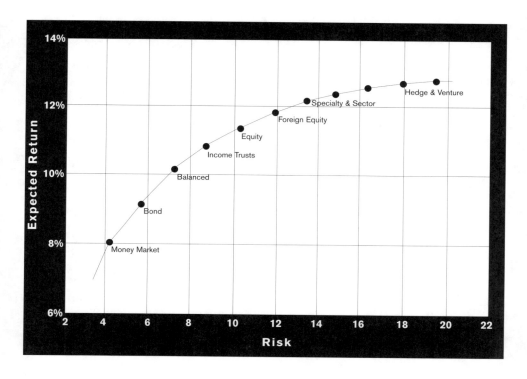

Key Points

- **Open-end funds** are more commonly held and (in general) offer **greater liquidity**.

- **Closed-end funds** can trade at **premiums** or **discounts** to their net asset value.

- There are generally **three types** of mutual funds: **Money Market**, **Bond**, and **Equity**. There are many variations on these three types.

- There are some **closed-end equity funds** that trade on the TSE with very **low management fees**. Information can be obtained on these funds through full-service brokers.

Chapter 2

A Short History of Mutual Funds

In order to get a better understanding of how a product works or how it performs, a look at the historical track record is often useful. While history is no predictor of future performance, it can often provide some revealing insights.

The Cyclical Nature of Mutual Fund Popularity

The first equity mutual fund in North America was created back in 1924 (it was of the closed-end variety). The 1920s are best remembered as a time of extreme lifestyles and of tremendous hope as America (and Canada) experienced phenomenal growth and increasing prosperity. The stock market was flying, and equity mutual funds provided a way of participating in that success. With the crash of 1929, most mutual funds vanished as the equity holdings that they had owned dropped as much as 90% in value. In fact, 90% of the funds that were available in the 1920s simply disappeared over the next decade. It was hard to manage money when there was no money left. (There were over 500 funds in the 1920s; that number had dropped to 68 by 1940.)

Mutual funds did survive, however, and by 1940 the industry had roughly $500 million under administration. It would not be until 1954 (25 years after the crash) that the Dow Jones Industrial Average got back to its 1929 high and it would take until the 1960s before mutual funds would really become a household item.

The 1960s would see explosive growth in mutual fund sales and performances. They are remembered as the "go-go" years and investing in the "nifty fifty" (America's up and coming companies at the time) was a so-called "no brainer". Successful fund managers became stars in their own right, as they are today. Investment in stocks and mutual funds gathered steam as the decade wore on, culminating in an enthusiastic peak in fund performance in 1968. The performance returns of the top 20 performing U.S. funds of 1968 had gains ranging from 30.4% to 90.1%, with an average gain of 45.7% per annum, according to James Stack, editor of InvestTech Research. In the bear market of 1969-1970, these same funds had a combined loss of 50.8%. In fact, of these funds, only 6 of the 20 still remained in 1993. What happened to the others is a good question. Many investors had significant losses, and the industry experienced some major scandals.

Interesting Historical Episodes

One of the most highly-publicized of these scandals involved an organization named IOS Limited, headed by Bernie Cornfeld (anybody who was around in the 1960s will remember the name). IOS Limited had a very large sales force that flogged funds by the truckload to large and small investors alike. Much of the fund money disappeared and confidence in mutual funds as a whole was badly shaken. The industry was, however, sufficiently mature and sufficiently regulated to survive. Despite the disappearance of many equity funds in the early- to mid-1970s, the number of money market and bond funds increased greatly in number and size. In the 1980s, with the exception of the 1987 crash (or "correction"), strong markets encouraged equity fund sales and the financial industry as a whole kept pace with the markets.

The growth in the 1990s is unparalleled and there are now over 7000 mutual funds that have in excess of $3.4 trillion in the U.S. alone. Many investors have achieved spectacular results. The question that must be now be asked is whether or not this sector can keep growing at this pace. Many brokers, salespeople and analysts now follow quite closely the monthly numbers of asset flows going into and coming out of funds. In fact, the *Investors Business Daily* even has a mutual fund index that charts the performance of 20 mutual funds in the U.S. With mutual fund holdings now making up a very large portion of the market, a drop in the amount invested in mutual funds each month may lead to a general market decline. Conversely, more money coming in may help the market to continue its incredible rise.

The graph below shows the increase in mutual fund assets during the 1990s in Canada.

THE INVESTMENT FUNDS INSTITUTE OF CANADA

Total Net Assets* Year End December, 1991 to 1996

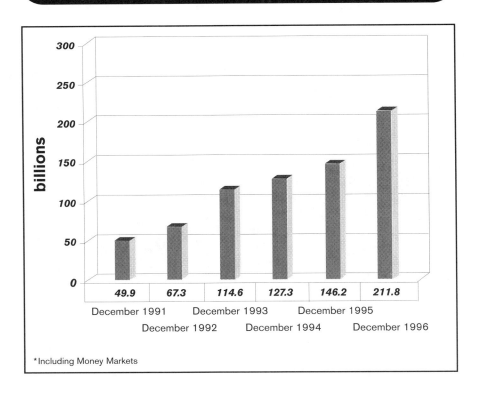

billions

| 49.9 | 67.3 | 114.6 | 127.3 | 146.2 | 211.8 |

December 1991   December 1993   December 1995
December 1992   December 1994   December 1996

*Including Money Markets

The mutual investor today must keep in mind that the stock market and equity mutual funds are a cyclical phenomenon. In general, equity mutual funds rise in number, assets and popularity in step with the equity market. This is borne out by an analysis of the historical performance of the stock market and equity mutual funds. Where we stand currently in the cycle will only be revealed in the years to come.

Key Points

- The **stock market** and the **mutual fund market** are **cyclical** in nature.

- Every time the markets rise to seemingly **unrealistic levels,** there are always those who say "**this time it's different**". They may be right, but **don't bet on it.**

Chapter 3

The Benefits of Mutual Funds

The many benefits that mutual funds offer can be grouped into four general categories:

- Diversification
- Low Initial Investment and Easy Record Keeping
- Professional Money Management
- Liquidity

Diversification

For the majority of investors, large sums of money would be needed to properly diversify a portfolio over different stocks and different asset classes. Asset class diversification is a wise practice because certain asset classes outperform others over different periods of time. Mutual funds offer diversification over many different markets and asset classes to investors who don't need to have great sums of money to buy units of the fund.

Assets can be divided into two main classes:

- **financial assets**, including cash, bonds, foreign currencies, and
- **hard assets**, including precious metals, real estate, commodities, etc.

Over time, the markets will value these two types of assets differently, some-times rewarding hard assets (e.g. during the real estate boom of the late 1980s in Canada and the U.S.) and sometimes favouring financial assets (e.g. cash or bonds) when high interest rates are coupled with low inflation.

Surprisingly enough, the concept of diversification is a relatively new invest-ment theory, stemming from an article by a graduate student, Harry Markowitz, at the University of Chicago back in 1952. He would go on to win a Nobel Prize for his theory in 1990. With the large increase in the number and types of mutual funds created recently, it is possible to properly diversify over many different asset classes. Furthermore, with assets properly diversified, the volatility of the portfolio will be greatly reduced. This is very important, as investors who are too heavily weighted in one area (usually stocks or equity mutual funds) can often become nervous and panic during turbulent times and unfortunately sell at precisely the wrong time. Proper asset allocation can help in avoiding this damaging behaviour.

While some argue that diversification only ensures mediocrity of investment return, nothing could be further from the truth when a good diversification strategy is properly implemented (see Chapter 16).

Low Initial Investment and Easy Record Keeping

Today's mutual fund companies have made it very easy for almost anyone to buy their products. Technology has reduced the cost of mutual fund transactions to the extent that many fund companies will allow minimum purchases of as low as $500 or even less. The small investor pays the same percentage charges as the large fundholder (e.g. a fixed rate of 2% of assets for management fees for equity funds) and is equally diversified. Trying to diversify your investments by yourself with $500 would be next to impossible. Most discount brokerage firms charge a minimum of $40 per transac-tion plus a fee for the number of shares bought or sold. If you invested only $500 under these circumstances, diversification would be impossible. Furthermore, most brokerage houses require a minimum of $1000 for bond or strip bond purchases; once again diversification would be impossible.

The fund companies also provide many services that make investing and record keeping easy:

- annual and semi-annual account statements that show the value of your holdings

- quarterly reports which update the investor as to the money manager's performance

- comments on the fund's present holdings as well as general comments about the current investment climate, and

- tax receipts which are broken down into realized capital gains and calculations of the dividends and interest earned over the twelve month tax year, which are easily entered on the fundholder's tax return for Revenue Canada.

Many fund companies even have withdrawal plans whereby money can be withdrawn from the fundholder's bank account on a monthly or quarterly basis, automatically allowing the investor to conveniently participate in the benefits of dollar cost averaging (see Chapter 16).

Professional Money Management

The investment world has changed dramatically over the past five to ten years. The changes that technology has brought about in the structure of business and in the way the economy functions have been dramatic. The old investment adage of "buy and hold good companies for the long term" can be seriously questioned today. Consider the fact that 40% of the Fortune 500 companies of 1950 are no longer in business. Equally noteworthy is the fact that several computer companies recently generated approximately 70% of their revenues from products that didn't even exist two years earlier. The product cycle in business has never been shorter. Companies that are industry leaders one day can become obsolete the next.

It can be stated that we are living in the information age, and it is certainly true that we have easy access to many new sources of information. At the same time, it is very difficult to determine which information is useful or accurate and how to apply it in a changing market environment. Mutual funds provide professional management where the money manager can devote all his or her time to tracking companies, interviewing company management and staying on top of market news to provide a superior rate of return for the investor. Whether the manager achieves this goal depends on several factors. Anyone considering buying a mutual fund should evaluate the fund manager's competence and investment track record.

Another factor favouring using professional money managers over trying to do it yourself are the complex accounting rules and practices used by many publicly traded companies. A trained professional is less likely to be fooled by the creative accounting practices in which some companies engage in their financial statements. While most companies are up front and forthright in their reporting of financial results, there are companies that do push the limits of the rules. Consider the following:

- Under GAAP (Generally Accepted Accounting Principles) companies have a lot of leeway in how they present their financial statements to investors and to others in the press and investment community. Financial statements can be more of an art than a science. It is often possible for a company to adjust expenses (known as capitalizing expenses) and report them as an asset (rather than an expense) on the balance sheet. This can increase the reported earnings of the company significantly and thus help the stock price rise (higher earnings usually boost the perceived value of a company). The company will then amortize or write off the cost of the expense over a period of up to as much as forty years. These actions help the company's performance over the shorter term, but can be disastrous over the longer term. Of course, the average shareholder will often be unaware that this game is going on.

- Another interesting fact is that the auditing firm hired by the company is required to sign the financial statements (meaning they approve the presentation of the numbers) and follow the policy of "true, fair and plain disclosure". The problem is that this leaves a lot of room for interpretation. It is no secret that landing an auditing job for a corporation is highly dependent on price. If a company is not willing to pay an adequate amount to have an audit performed, it may not be possible for the accounting firm to do a thorough audit of the company. In many instances the auditor must rely solely on what the company tells them. Unfortunately, in some situations this can lead to less-than-adequate audit results. As amazing as it sounds, there have been companies (primarily in the U.S.) that have reported consistent growth in earnings over a number of years and then suddenly filed for Chapter 11 bankruptcy protection against their creditors one financial quarter later. Quite often the major shareholder or shareholders in this situation have made more money selling their stock into the market than the company could ever have dreamed of making in the normal course of its business. As a result, many class action suits have been brought against company directors and auditors by shareholders.

There is some merit to these criticisms. Some of the largest computer companies in the U.S. have come under harsh criticism on the subject of share buy-backs of company stock by the company, and excessive stock option issuance to top executives. The company often pays less in salaries to these executives, thereby lowering expenses and raising earnings. These types of executive stock options do not show up in the accounting numbers. The trading of listed stock options by the company on behalf of the company of its own listed options (puts and calls) is also part of this game. Recently, this type of trading has accounted for a significant percentage of several well-known companies' annual incomes. The complaints are that too much attention is paid to the short-term movements of the stock and not enough attention is paid to the business fundamentals.

A good fund manager (it is hoped) will be able to identify, and avoid, the kinds of companies that have questionable earnings. That can be very difficult even for well-trained managers because so little information is actually provided. That information can also be very selective at times, and might consist only of the good news that the company wants people to see.

Finally, another real benefit to professionally-managed money (in this case relating to stocks) is that good money managers can find very good companies that are often faceless until much later on in their growth cycle when the bigger firms on Wall Street or Bay Street or the investing public finally take notice. There is little doubt that the fund managers who invested early in companies like Nike (which went public in 1980), or Microsoft (which went public in 1986) did terrifically well for the funds they managed and added real value for the shareholder. The average investor would need a very good broker, or salesperson, or knowledgeable sources to compete in the growth stock area (which is where most of the really spectacular gains are often made) and come out ahead.

A note of caution concerning professional money management should be sounded here. In issue 1223 of Richard Russell's "*Dow Theory Letters*" (April 9, 1997) the average age of today's money manager is reported to be 29.5 years. This statistic comes from a survey done by the American Funds Group on a group of 7000 mutual fund managers in the U.S. The latter organization also found that these managers had an average of no more than 3.5 years of experience! If these statistics are reliable, then it must be true that very few money managers have ever managed money in a downward moving, or "bear" market. In fact, of the 7000 managers surveyed, only 14% had experienced the bear market of 1973-74, and only 20% were around for the crash of 1987. How the majority of these young managers may react to future market adversity is an interesting, and perhaps frightening thought. It is particularly alarming when one considers that 90% of all money in mutual funds today has only been invested since 1990. In chapter 4 I will present certain methods of evaluating a mutual fund and its managers in order to protect yourself from problems that can arise from a money manager's lack of experience.

Liquidity

One of the great benefits of owning mutual funds is their liquidity. For open-end funds, a redemption notice or sell order is entered and in most cases the fundholder gets the value of the fund at its closing price that day (some funds are valued weekly or monthly). There are usually no fees associated with this transaction (aside from some special cases, i.e., deferred sales charges when completely cashing out of a family of funds) and the fundholder is usually entitled to his or her money after the common three-day settlement. With closed-end funds an order must be placed through a broker or licensed salesperson, and a buyer for the security must be found. In most cases this presents no problem. However, there may at times be a wide spread between the bid price and the ask price. For example, the buyer for the fund unit may be willing to pay $9.75 while the current offer price on the fund is $10. In order for the seller to get out of the position, he or she would have to "hit", or take, the bid price, at $9.75, which in this case would be a 2.5% difference from the $10 offer. Factor in commissions of, say, 2% for the broker, and the closed-end fund is much less liquid than the open-ended one. Furthermore, the closed-end fund may at the time be trading at a discount (to its real net asset value) which might cause further losses in real terms to the seller.

The importance of having liquidity in investments cannot be overstated. Investors who bought into real estate in the late 1980s know first hand how difficult life can be when you are unable to get out of an investment. At times, houses and office buildings can sit with no bids or buyers on the horizon for long periods of time. Couple this with potential carrying costs and other taxes, and firesale prices are accepted for assets, in order to prevent bankruptcy. Potential buyers will often know the predicaments of the seller and will be able to wait them out to extract the lowest price possible.

A discussion of real estate illiquidity is relevant when considering what happened to several prominent open-end realty mutual funds after the price collapse in this sector in the early 1990s. While bankruptcy of a fund is near impossible (without using leverage the price can only go down to zero), these mutual funds faced massive redemption notices as the funds' real estate asset values dropped. Because the funds didn't have enough cash on hand to handle the sell orders, and selling the real estate properties quickly was next to impossible, the fund managers decided to prevent any more redemption orders by removing the ability of fundholders to sell, so that investors were locked in. It has only been recently that these funds have begun trading again, most of them being converted to closed-end funds so that the managers have a fixed amount of money to work with and won't have to sell realty holdings when a fundholder wants to get out.

Equity mutual funds (which invest mainly in stocks) offer excellent liquidity and fundholders can generally move from one fund to another within a fund family (usually at no cost). An investor who buys equities on his or her own account faces a transaction cost on every transaction (which can really add up). Because mutual funds are so large, their relative transaction costs, in percentage terms, are much less than those paid by individual investors.

Most of the time, liquidity is not a problem (especially for bond and money market funds), but special circumstances can arise when liquidity, specifically on equities, can dry up. In falling markets, there are times when stock prices can drop very quickly. October of 1987 is a good example. The market plunged over 500 points in New York (a 22% drop in its value) in a single day. For periods of time, there were no bids at all on many stocks. Market makers, who are employed by brokerage houses and whose responsibility it is to ensure a market exists in given stocks, simply stepped away from trying to support the prices and instead let them fall. (The best analogy that comes to mind is getting out of the way of a speeding freight train.)

One should also consider that market makers are trying to make money for their respective employers, while making markets in these stocks. You don't make money buying shares while the price keeps dropping! During the crisis and chaos of 1987, one fund company's phone lines went down for several days and many investors couldn't get through to sell their existing shares. These are circumstances when lack of liquidity (and/or access to liquidity) can seriously hurt fundholders, often before they even know it.

Since 1987 the stock exchanges have brought in rules (e.g. restrictions on computerized trading after a particular market drops to a certain level etc.) to try to prevent a recurrence of the kind of extreme fluctuation seen in 1987. Fund companies also currently have policies in place to alleviate some of these potential problems. For example, it is possible for fund management to borrow against the value of the mutual fund to obtain cash to deal with heavy redemption orders. The fund is then required to pay back the loan (over a certain number of days) by selling stocks into the market under hopefully more stable circumstances. It should be noted that this situation is by no means the norm and happens very infrequently. My intent in mentioning such situations is simply to point out the possible problems that may arise for the owners of mutual funds. Having said that, advanced planning should be able to prevent a liquidity crisis from hurting you if you own mutual funds, and it may even help you to profit from a market that is heading downwards.

Key Points

- Mutual funds offer investors the ability to **diversify** over many different asset classes and markets with **small** initial and subsequent **investments.**

- The fund companies do most of the **record keeping**, and keep track of capital gains, and dividend and interest income earned within the fund.

- **Professional money management** is provided by the fund company to the investor. The fund company generally has a better **working knowledge of the markets** and many more resources at its disposal for successful market investment.

- The **liquidity** provided through mutual fund ownership (particularly open-ended funds) is excellent and would otherwise be very difficult to achieve for small and medium sized investors.

Chapter 4

Things You Should Know About Today's Equity Mutual Funds

It is very difficult to put into proper perspective what is actually happening in the equity mutual fund industry today. Management companies and the investment industry are portraying equity mutual funds as a good long-term investment that will lead to much better results than if you don't participate in the stock markets. Funds are depicted as a hands-off investment where the investor can feel confident that a professional is managing the investments and will achieve superior rates of return. Is this a realistic expectation? Perhaps. However, there are a few questions that investors should ask themselves before making any decisions on investing.

What Rate of Return Should Be Expected?

A relatively recent survey done by an organization called Marketing Solutions Inc. indicated that approximately 50% of respondents expected a 10-12% rate of return or better on equity funds. Is this expectation too high? In most cases it is, particularly over a longer period of time. However, when investors inquire about funds or see the funds' advertisements, they are generally only presented with the performance figures of the better funds. It's only natural that companies would advertise their best performing funds and downplay the others. Advertising will also quite often cater to the fad at the time. Mutual fund investing in German equities became all the rage when the Berlin Wall came down in 1989. Unfortunately, most of the funds' values also came down after the hype subsided and the reality of the unification costs became apparent. Next was a surge of investment in the Far East, because of the positive reforms and moves towards developing more capitalistic societies in China and neighbouring countries. These developments may be ongoing, but the bloom is off the rose after share prices and mutual fund performance failed to live up to expectations. Particularly interesting were the rates of return seen on mutual funds invested in Latin America. Many fund companies had spectacular rates of return from their specialty funds investing in Latin America, which were followed by large advertising campaigns. After the devaluation of the Mexican peso in late 1994 and early 1995, many of these funds plunged 40% to 50% in the span of just a few weeks. Following this, the advertisements regarding the wonderful growth potential in this yet untapped area dried up. To be fair, not all fund companies take this approach to marketing (and in reality there is nothing wrong with it if it is factual). However it is imperative that the fund buyer knows about this type of marketing and realizes how compelling it can be.

The people who sell and distribute equity mutual funds may also give rise to inflated expectations among fund investors. Charts and graphs showing how much better stocks and equity mutual funds have done over the last 40 years (as compared with treasury bills, bonds and inflation) are often presented to potential fund purchasers. Some salespeople will actually encourage clients to borrow money (or use leverage) in order to purchase more funds. The purported rationale for this is that the funds will outperform the interest costs of the loan, which can then be written off on the investor's tax bill (the interest costs, that is). This is a very dangerous process based on some faulty assumptions. For every positive statistic presented to an investor on mutual fund and stock market performance over a certain period, there is usually a counterbalancing warning statistic that could be presented.

What Are the Risks Involved?

This is a very interesting question. There are risks associated with both being "in the market" (i.e., investing in equities) and not being in the market. Inflation and taxes are the two variables that ultimately decide whether an investment has been a success or a failure. By staying in treasury bills all the time, there is a very good chance that the investment will actually give a negative real rate of return because of inflation and the investor will lose purchasing power. By investing in equities or equity mutual funds (where both capital gains and gains from dividends are taxed at a lower rate) it is likely that, over a longer period of time, investors will achieve positive real rates of return on their money. This is not always true, as there have been instances (not too long ago both in Canada and the U.S.) where investments in equities and equity funds lost 75% of their real value over an extended period of time. Specifically, this occurred in the U.S. between 1966 and 1984.

Therefore, when putting money into equity mutual funds, the investor has to be cognisant of the problems associated with equity investments (i.e., that their values fluctuate over different time periods). These problems can be minimized through investment strategies that allow the investor periodic investments in many different markets through the use of dollar cost averaging (see Chapter 16).

Another even more potentially dangerous risk can be the complacency of the investor. In the last several years, the major banks in Canada have moved heavily into the financial services arena through purchases of the formerly large and independent brokerage companies. They have also put a major emphasis on managed money services down at the branch level. Most bank employees have either taken, or are working on "The Canadian Investment Funds Course" which, if completed successfully, allows them to sell mutual funds to bank customers. While the banks do provide in-house training on their products, in reality, one course allows their employees to sell quite complex investments to investors that are, in most cases, unsophisticated. In addition, investors who view the banks as stable and conservative institutions may be under the assumption that their investments are rock solid and safe, when this may not be the case. In fact, a few years ago a study indicated that many mutual fund buyers thought that their mutual funds were insured under the CDIC (Canada Deposit Insurance Corporation). Of course, that is not the case. It is not inconceivable that a downturn in the stock markets in the future would result in a number of lawsuits.

Each province in Canada has a body to regulate its investment industry. The Ontario Securities Commission (OSC) has recently taken a more active role, for better or for worse, in regulating the way the mutual fund industry operates. Although this may make investors feel a sense of security, the idea that a regulatory agency will ensure that investors don't get hurt, in my opinion, could not be further from the truth. Although it is now true that the risk features of the investment must be clearly spelled out in its prospectus document, unfortunately most people don't even read this document (mainly because, until recently, prospectuses have been written in a way that is very difficult to understand). When selling mutual funds, the broker, distributor or salesperson has an obligation to spell out all the risks, although it is quite likely that they themselves have very little idea of what all the risks are. (The "know your client rule" requires the broker or salesperson to understand the client's needs, wants, risk tolerance, level of knowledge etc., so that appropriate investments may be recommended and purchased. It is the most important rule governing the securities industry.) Currently, the banking and brokerage industry is implementing more and more educational courses to increase the level of understanding of the people who are licensed to sell mutual fund products.

Do You Know What You Are Investing In?

It is amazing that people can work so hard in life to make a decent wage and yet when it comes to actually investing what they have left over after taxes and necessary expenses, they show so little interest in the process. Granted, most people don't have a lot of time for this exercise, and letting someone else manage your money can save time. However, investors must remember that it is *their* money and only they can really know what is best for them. Consider this: in most cases investors have no real idea who is managing their money. It's probably not enough just to know the name and track record of your money manager. A lot of trust is invested in the money manager. That person might by all accounts be very good, but he or she may be doing things with your money that you yourself might never, ever consider. True, he or she is supposed to operate under the investment guidelines in the fund's prospectus, but quite often these requirements leave a lot of room for manoeuvring. While not trying to overstate the point, does anyone think that the residents of Orange County, California (the infamously bankrupt county) knew that their municipal government was buying and selling interest rate options and futures with their municipal funds before it went bankrupt? And if they had known, wouldn't they have thought that the person controlling the money knew what he was doing? And if he didn't know what he was doing, the brokerage firm that was selling him on the idea would have known what it was doing, right? Wrong. It is quite likely that this situation would not have happened if each resident was managing his or her own portion of the money individually. But, because the manager of the fund and the brokerage house didn't have his own money in it, greater liberties were taken. This point is presented to highlight the fact that it is essential that investors know what they own and that they are always on guard to ensure that their best interests are being served.

Today's Investment Scene

There is a tremendous amount of information about equity mutual funds and stock markets coming at us from all directions these days. The larger newspapers often have two or three articles a day on mutual funds and usually include an entire section each week dedicated to mutual funds. There are nightly business shows that describe the day's action on the markets, with a variety of guests on the shows, each of whom has various opinions on what it all means. 24-hour television programs (largely sponsored by the investment industry) such as CNBC are available to bring a constant supply of information to investors. The constant flow of news, and the stock price ticker tapes running continuously along the bottom of the screen, generate an atmosphere of energy and excitement.

If you subscribe to any of the numerous investment newsletters available, you're probably constantly bombarded by other newsletter organizations' advertisements (they frequently purchase subscriber lists from one another) that seem to have outstanding ideas and promises. "**$10,000 turned into $186,000 — $6,000 turned into $305,000. Total return on two investments: $491,000 in just five years!**" is an example of one I recently received in the mail. It has often been said that two forces drive the markets: greed and fear. It is quite obvious which emotion the above example is trying to elicit. The next newsletter you receive is just as likely to read: "**How to prepare yourself for the upcoming depression,**" offering to help you (if you subscribe to the newsletter) through the dark days ahead.

The number of investment "clubs" has skyrocketed recently. This fact could be a good contrary indicator for the future performance of the markets. At the meetings of these clubs, ideas and information are discussed by the members and then certain decisions are acted upon. Probably the most interesting new medium for information dissemination is the Internet. Two young men have recently created a Web site called the *"Motley Fool,"* where computer types and investors alike can log on and exchange information about the goings-on in the investment market. The fascinating part of it all is the number of subscribers (in the tens of thousands) and how influential this group can actually be upon markets. On various occasions, stocks have moved quite dramatically after being mentioned or discussed on this Web site. While the focus for this group has generally been the hi-tech sector, there has been some spillover into other markets.

There is little doubt, from examining past statistics, that the mutual fund industry is highly cyclical. Specifically, the number of mutual funds available correlates highly with stock market performance. The better the market, the greater the number of mutual funds. And as the market subsequently declines, the number of mutual funds declines with it. One indicator that is currently being watched closely by many market participants is the money flow into mutual funds. Marc Faber, a well-respected Hong Kong newsletter writer, has tracked the flows in and out of equity markets and believes there is a natural tendency for the public to buy when markets are high and sell when they are low.

In the 1970s, when the markets were low, there were continuous redemptions by private investors. Shortly before the crash of 1987, there was a big upturn in mutual fund inflows, and just before the recovery in 1988, there were large outflows. Faber's data indicates that most investors tend to start to participate in the market usually about two years after it has begun (studies reveal that $1/3$ of a bull market move often occurs in the first four months). As a result, most investors tend to miss a large part, if not all, of the gains. If one accepts Faber's position, then it may seem logical to assume that, because of the large flow of money into mutual funds at present, we may be near the top in terms of stock market pricing and valuations.

It has become increasingly difficult, however, to accept the predictive assumptions of public buying and selling behaviour regarding the equity markets of the 1990s because of the fact that markets have been so strong for such a long period of time with massive public involvement. How is it, with the Dow cracking the 4000 level in February of 1995, with large public money inflows, it registered a 50% gain and soared to well over 6000 in less than two years? And, after a little more than two years, it cracked 8000 in 1997! Maybe the public got it right!

Will the Upward Trend in Equity Markets Continue?

At present, equity markets in North America seem to be overvalued by just about every yardstick traditionally used in market analysis. This is not to say that the markets will come down in the near future or that they can't go a lot higher. While stock prices are ultimately driven by earnings and dividends, in the short term they can be affected by emotions (i.e., greed and fear), or the hyped potential future prospects of a company. In a strong market, a company's future prospects can be grossly exaggerated or overly optimistic, which will usually be reflected in the stock price. Investors pay a lot for the expectation that they will be rewarded a few years down the road. If the company's prospects start to fade, or a new or better competitor comes along, the share price can implode. The opposite is true in a recession or a bear market where a quality company may be undervalued because there are very few expectations of good times down the road.

All this means that it is very important that the equity mutual fund investor understand the stock market sentiment when venturing into the investment ring. There is a natural tendency in life to expect that things in their present state will continue indefinitely. I heard a good example of this kind of thinking at a recent seminar at which the speaker mentioned the story of Charles H. Duell, the U.S. Commissioner of Patents in 1899. At that time, Mr. Duell suggested to Congress that the patent office shut down because everything that needed to be invented had already been invented! While corporate downsizing and shakeouts may have tempered people's belief in continuity, trying to foresee change is still difficult. It is often easier to explain the *status quo*, and to justify its continuation.

A good example of this is provided by a recent mutual fund guide book in which the authors declare that we are in a new era, the "era of managed money". They go on to explain how this came to be, although they make no attempt to explain to the reader that the popularity of mutual funds has waxed and waned throughout their history (see Chapter 2). The reader of the above-mentioned guide is not provided with a balanced view, and could wander into dangerous investment decisions without being armed with complete information.

Other recent examples of this kind of thinking come to mind. In the late 1980s, the Japanese stock market was trading, by all standards, at dizzying heights.

At the time, however, there were a number of reasons that supposedly justified those levels: the Japanese tax rules were different, the markets were rigged (i.e., there was a lot of cross-ownership of Japanese companies who invested in each other's shares) and Japan had a highly controlled economy. It was only after the bubble burst that it became obvious to all that the market had in fact been overvalued. The Toronto real estate market at that same time is another good example. It was often argued that real estate prices would never come down because Toronto was an international city, and the continued influx of Hong Kong dollars would keep prices rising. Today, real estate prices are below their 1989 high, and real estate currently does not offer the great speculative investment opportunities that it once did.

Watch Out for the Theories

Today, some of the theories that explain the popularity of stock markets and equity mutual funds are indeed similar to those that explained the rising real estate market of the 1980s. For many years people believed that their home was the best investment, as its price would rise with, or outperform, inflation and that a house was a good way to engage in "forced savings". (Remember the line "Why pay rent to someone when you can pay yourself?") The truth of the matter *now* is that people who have been renting for the last ten years (instead of speculating in real estate or buying in the late 1980s) are the winners. Mutual fund ownership may now be filling the home's former role in many people's minds as the best way of providing for the future and hedging against inflation.

An interesting article published in a recent issue of *Harper's Magazine* tells the story of a man with financial woes who hopes to extricate himself by investing in equity mutual funds. Being in his early forties, he realistically sees little hope in his current financial situation and cannot foresee himself being able to retire comfortably. He explains that he is now basically going to roll the dice and hopes that the equity markets will bail him out. The article was written by the magazine's business writer. His attitude may help in explaining why gambling casinos are becoming so popular!

Interestingly, the study of demographics has also recently become popular in predicting future trends in consumer wants and needs, and currently is being applied to investing in the stock market. It is argued that by following the growth stages of the baby boomers (those born roughly between 1947 and 1966), one can predict which industries will do well as the boomers reach each different life cycle. Currently, the boomers are in their savings cycle after having bought houses (which might explain why the real estate prices have risen and fallen) and mutual funds and stocks will do well as this new cycle of investing still has a long way to go. This is interesting stuff. We should remember, however, that this is only a theory and may not apply in every circumstance. Often, the theory is applied to events that have already happened and thus its effectiveness in predicting future behaviour can be questioned. In fact, one of the well-known supporters of demographic predictive theory suggested to me in the late 1980s that I should buy cottage property as an investment. His idea was that the boomers had bought their homes and that cottage prices would rise since cottages would be their next big investment. I'm rather glad I didn't take his advice as cottage property prices haven't really moved at all in the last seven years (in fact a lot of these properties have gone down in value).

The Japanese equity mutual fund market provides another interesting illustration of the drawbacks of demographic theory. The Japanese are an older population than North Americans and they save money at twice the rate that we do. Surprisingly, from 1990 to 1996 the number of assets owned by the Japanese in the form of Japanese equity mutual funds has dropped approximately 91%! Where has the money gone? Although we can't say for sure, what we can say is that a greater rate of savings does not necessarily mean that equity mutual fund or stock prices will rise.

Some people say that another reason that equity markets will continue to rise for the next ten to twenty years is that there will be continuing inter-generational wealth transfer. The statistics reveal that boomers will receive very large inheritances over the next two decades and a recent survey indicates that a majority of respondents said that they will invest this money in the equity markets. This seems like a reasonable response now, but will these people still feel the same way if equity markets underperform for the next five years? As well, with one stroke of the pen, the Canadian government could bring in wealth taxes (which the U.S. government has already done) to help pay down the debt, and finance many of the other unfunded liabilities that don't show up in regular government reporting but must still be paid for. This great wealth transfer may look more like a slow drip to the inheritors if the government can't solve its current fiscal problems with current laws and tax policies.

Some Popular Sales Pitches

Invest In Funds For The Long Term

It has never been easier for the financial services industry to sell mutual funds on the merits of their performance. Looking at the performance numbers of many funds over the past 1, 3, 5 and possibly even 10 years, it may appear that investing in mutual funds over the long term is essential for success. But is it?

Much of the marketing literature and presentations directed at the public portray mutual funds as an investment for the long term. This is undoubtedly sound advice. No one should invest in mutual funds for quick market gains (the equity markets are much too unpredictable). The performance numbers presented today, however, may be a bit misleading due to the effects of end term bias. End term bias is the tendency of recent returns to help lift the longer term numbers to higher levels. As a result of the strong equity market performance in recent years, this has had a significant impact on many of the funds' longer term track records. Similar data on bond performance in past years (if the presenter chooses the best performance time period) can show equally attractive results for bond investments. Be aware!

Selling Funds Through The Guise Of Financial and Retirement Planning

Financial and retirement planning are hot subjects today. One of the major thrusts of advertising and marketing to the public is to "get one's financial house in order and start planning for retirement". A common theme today is that government isn't going to have enough money in future years to help its elderly citizens to retire to the lifestyle that they desire. "You're going to outlive your money" is also a catch-phrase that, much like the previous statement, undoubtedly has some validity, and the power of this suggestion does cause one to think. The idea of establishing a financial plan definitely makes sense, but one must be careful to sort the wheat from the chaff.

The advertising and promotional seminars that emphasize the importance of financial planning are frequently given or sponsored by individuals or companies that earn much of their income or revenue from the sale of mutual funds. When a financial strategy is given, mutual fund ownership quite often makes up a large part of the financial "plan". One should seriously question this.

For the majority of individuals, any financial strategy other than paying down your home mortgage, topping up your RRSPs, owning adequate life and health insurance, paying off outstanding debts and reinvesting what is left, should be seriously questioned. How is it realistically possible to set up a complex financial plan when every year (or with every federal budget), the government changes the tax laws, the RRSP contribution limits (some years they may actually not!) and a host of other things that make planning out more than one year next to impossible. How many retirement plans were dramatically altered for retired Canadians following the government clawback of Old Age Security in recent years? Could anyone, in all honesty, have predicted its implementation and had the foresight or the ability (or the cash for that matter) to cushion its blow to the pocketbook? In all likelihood, not many people could have.

Mutual funds can have an important role in financial planning, but understanding how that role is best suited to you is essential.

Understanding the Economics

Some of the other reasons that are currently used to explain stock market and equity mutual fund popularity and success are: the low interest rates that are offered today, good economic growth, successful corporate restructurings that have made North American companies the envy of the industrialized world, and low inflation. These are valid reasons for wanting to have a stake in good stocks and equity funds at this time but the point must be made that market conditions and sentiment may change (quite possibly very quickly) and investors need to be prepared.

When we look behind the low inflation numbers that are currently given in the form of the CPI (Consumer Price Index), we can actually see that, in other ways, there is currently a tremendous level of inflation. This inflation is reflected in the high prices that are being paid for equities, specifically the higher prices being paid to buy $1 worth of the earnings of a company. Kurt Richenbacher, in the September 1996 issue of *The Richenbacher Letter*, points out that the market value of American equities has increased $5 trillion over the last six years without a corresponding percentage increase in earnings (60% earnings growth over the past six years). Thus, investors are paying much more for stocks to get the same dollar's worth of earnings, indicating that there is tremendous asset inflation. Upon further examination of the earnings growth, he claims that the productivity of American companies improved only marginally over this time, and that lower interest rates, lower corporate taxes and lower contributions to company pension plans were the major reason for the profit increases. If any one of these situations changes, which sooner or later they must, in one form or another, he claims that huge asset price drops will occur.

Interest rates have been quite low in recent years. It is arguable that this is a result of foreign banks (primarily the bank of Japan), buying U.S. bonds and dollars to strengthen the U.S. dollar and make foreign producers' products cheaper to American consumers. (Japan has been mired in a recession/depression for the past 5 years). How long this foreign buying and support can continue is anyone's guess, but one thing is certain: it will not go on forever. If interest rates subsequently rise in the U.S. (through natural market forces and/or by the selling of U.S. dollars and bonds by foreign banks), then the U.S. economy may experience some real problems. Declining valuations of North American equity prices may anticipate or follow this eventuality.

The above discussion certainly does not aim to scare people into inaction, or to encourage pessimism. Rather, it is intended to point out views that are not often published in the popular press. Successful investing is a difficult and complex process that is not always rewarding, particularly for the investor who mistimes his or her investments.

Two Time-Tested Measurements

Trying to determine whether a market is cheap or expensive is a very difficult task. This is because the value given to a specific stock usually reflects the future potential of the company as opposed to the past or present performance of the company. The future movement of the stock will eventually reflect these expectations and whether or not they are met. There are two useful measurements that can be used in attempting to value a stock or a market based upon historical relationships. They are the Price/Earnings Multiple (or Ratio) and the Dividend Yield or Price/Dividend Multiple.

Unfortunately, markets may remain overpriced or undervalued for long periods of time, so that the predictive value of these measurements over the shorter term may be inadequate or even useless. Over the longer haul, if one doesn't believe in the "this time it's different" school of thought, these indicators will prove to be, in many cases, good measurement tools for the future direction of the market.

Price Earnings Multiple or Ratio

The price earnings (P/E) multiple or ratio compares the stock price of a company to its earnings for (usually) the most recent four quarters. For example, a company with a share price of $15 with $1 of earnings for the past four quarters would have a P/E of 15. The P/E ratio indicates what the market is willing to pay for $1 worth of earnings. (It is worth noting that many Wall Street and Bay Street analysts will often quote a P/E multiple based upon their future earnings projections for the company or companies followed. In these instances, the P/E numbers will tend to be lower and more attractive to the investor because they are based on higher earnings numbers which have been forecast for the upcoming years.)

The equity markets have generally averaged a P/E of 14 over the long term, so this number may lead one to conclude that the market may be overvalued by historic terms if the market averages a P/E of over 14 and undervalued or inexpensive if under 14. When market P/Es get much above this level, it may represent excessive optimism and be used as a warning system or red flag to investors. Conversely, when P/Es drop much below this level, it can reflect excessive pessimism about the company's or stock market's future, and may represent a good buying opportunity.

The P/E ratio for present markets (July 1997) are on the high side with 21.88 for the Dow Industrial, 23.55 for the S&P 500, 47 for the NASDAQ and 25.47 for the TSE 300. The NASDAQ market (National Association of Securities Dealers Automated Quotes system) has grown tremendously in number of stocks and volume of trading over the past decade and is home to many of America's largest computer and computer-related companies (e.g. Microsoft, Dell and Netscape). It currently trades at an incredible 47 P/E multiple. To put this number into better perspective, it would take a doubling of earnings of all stocks on this exchange to bring the P/E multiple to 23.5. While this may be possible (although highly unlikely in the near future), it would still be trading at a very high historical multiple. *Caveat emptor.*

Dividend Yield or the Price Dividend Multiple

The dividend yield relates the price of a stock to its dividend payout. If one divides the dividend by the stock price, the dividend yield is obtained. Conversely, if one divides the stock price by the dividend, the price dividend ratio is obtained.

The dividend yield on a stock is quite significant as it represents a hard cash on cash return from the investment. Currently, the Dow Industrial dividend yield is at an all-time low of 1.61% as is the S&P 500 at 1.61% (July 1997). The last time both of these indicators got close to these levels, they signalled a market top. The S&P 500 hit a low of 2.7% in 1929 and another low at 2.4% in 1987. Using the S&P 500 performance numbers from 1926 to 1992, the average annual rate of return for common stocks has been 10.5%.[1] Of this return, 4.7% or roughly 45% of this gain is directly attributable to the dividend payout. Therefore, the importance of dividends on equity performance is not easily dismissed. Today's markets, as one can see, are not paying much in dividends.

Many analysts do not attach as much importance to dividend yields as they once did. This is difficult to understand when one considers how important dividends have been to long-term rates of return on equities. One common argument is that many companies are retaining much of their earnings to help finance future growth opportunities. Analysts concur with this practice, feeling this money is better put to use by the company than by its shareholders. But for many of the largest companies in the U.S., most of which are operating in mature industries, the low dividend yields on these stocks are not as easily dismissed.

Key Points

- Approach mutual fund investing with **reasonable expectations** about your rate of return.

- Be aware that you are frequently being shown only the **best performance numbers** in mutual fund company **brochures and advertisements**. They rarely talk about their poor performers.

- The **timing** of your mutual fund purchase is critical to the return you will receive. The "buy now and forget about it" attitude may not be appropriate in today's investment world. A poorly-timed fund purchase can take years to correct itself.

- Remember that **it's your money**. You (not the salesperson) are the one with the greatest **vested interest** in a mutual fund's rate of return.

- **Know what you are buying** and make sure it is in line with your **risk tolerance**. You are the one assuming the risk of the fund, not the fund company or the fund manager.

- **Equity markets** are currently trading at **very high valuations** historically and you should **proceed with caution**. Do not invest in equity markets for the sole reason that bond and GIC rates are too low.

- **Question all theories and predictions** regarding markets and mutual funds. One thing is for sure: no one knows what direction the markets may go. No one.

- **Be aware** of the **popular sales pitches**. They are not necessarily true for your specific situation.

- Two time-tested market measurements, the **P/E ratio** and the **Stock Dividend Yield** can help put a **historical value** on the markets.

Notes:

[1] John C. Bogle, *Bogle on Mutual Funds,* p. 12. New York: Dell Publishing.

Chapter 5

Who Sells Equity Mutual Funds and How Are They Regulated?

A recent Price Waterhouse survey found that over 5 million Canadian adults, or about 26% of the population over 18 years of age, invest in mutual funds. This amazing statistic indicates the importance of the mutual fund industry and its increasing significance in the economy and the lives of individual Canadians. There are a number of different ways in which investors can purchase mutual funds. Some of the more common channels of distribution are mentioned below.

Investment funds in Canada are sold primarily through members of the Investment Dealers Association (IDA). This group includes members of the stock exchanges in Canada, banks, trust companies, and mutual fund dealers (some independent, others tied to the fund manager and described as a direct sales force). It should be mentioned that there are currently over 500 non-IDA firms selling mutual funds in Canada. In some cases, the fund is sold directly to the public by fund personnel. Insurance companies also offer many different mutual fund products in addition to the insurance and annuity products for which they are more commonly known. The purchase of U.S. mutual fund products is also possible through several channels, described later on in this chapter.

A short description of each of the above-mentioned distributors is in order.

In This Chapter:

- **Members of the Stock Exchanges**
- **Banks**
- **Trust Companies**
- **Mutual Fund Companies**
- **Independently-Owned Financial Service Companies**
- **Insurance Agents**
- **Buying U.S. Mutual Funds**
- **Key Points**

Members of the Stock Exchanges

Most full-service brokerage firms with seats on the different Canadian exchanges offer a wide variety of mutual funds. In fact, the amount of research, staff and money that these houses have invested in developing their mutual fund departments has increased steadily throughout the 1990s. Generally, the investment representatives or brokers employed by these firms have the ability to pick and choose the funds they wish to sell within given parameters. In most cases, these representatives or brokers will (naturally) favour mutual funds with front- or back-end commissions over funds that have a no-load structure. However, many brokers and their firms do have the ability to purchase no-load funds on behalf of their clients and hold them in the client's account at the full-service firm. Many of the no-load funds have a "trailer fee" structure. A broker will often take an order for a no-load fund in order to receive this trailer fee. By simply holding the fund, the broker will receive as much as 0.5% to 1.5%, or sometimes even more, of the value of the client's investment per year. (See Chapter 7, "**Mutual Fund Sales Charges and Fees**".)

Commission fees paid upon the purchase of front-end load mutual funds at full-service firms can often be negotiated by the client to a level that is acceptable to both parties. If the client does much of the homework and research independently, it is fair to ask for a lower commission rate on the purchase. On the other hand, if the client requires a lot of advice and relies more heavily on the broker for investment research and advice, it is reasonable for the broker to receive a greater fee for any transactions. This process involves a give and take between client and broker and the details should be agreed upon early on in the relationship. A happy client-broker relationship usually opens the way to improved service and more successful investment.

Discount brokerage houses will buy mutual funds for clients, usually charging a front-end fee of about 2% (although a back-end load arrangement is also possible). A wide variety of funds are generally available for purchase through these discount brokerage houses. Of course, it is assumed that the client knows what he or she wants because the discount firms make it clear that they do not offer investment advice. The annual trailer fees that would usually go to the salesperson on fund purchases are not applicable in this case. The discount firm receives the fees directly from the fund companies, as long as the funds continue to be held at the discount brokerage.

Banks

In recent years, the banks have become major players in the mutual fund and money management arena. Even factoring out the fact that the major five Canadian banks have all bought control of a major brokerage firm (except TD, which chose an alternative route, creating both a discount and a full-service department) the banks at the branch level have steadily grown their in-house mutual fund sales business.

All the banks offer their own mutual funds, which can be bought at the branch level, often in a separate area set aside for that purpose within the branch. In general these funds have no in or out commissions. Bank employees are encouraged to take the Canadian Investment Funds Course so that they can provide informed recommendations to customers who ask for advice on this subject. Several banks have recently brought in personnel at the branch level whose specific job description is to approach existing clients and sell them on the benefits of bank-managed money products. A real emphasis has been placed on this area as the margins are considerably larger on mutual funds than on short-term deposits or treasury bills. One area of concern that arises from this situation is that many bank customers, who have traditionally stayed with low-risk or risk-free investments such as GICs, are now invested in equity based funds that could fluctuate tremendously in value.

Many of these individuals have undoubtedly seen the impressive track records that certain funds have had over recent years. But how would they react if their particular funds were to drop sharply, or slowly drift down, over several months or years? Granted, the licensed sales people are governed by the "know your client" rule, meaning that they must understand the client's needs, goals, risk tolerance etc. The fact that a bank's name is behind a particular fund might lead to a false sense of security for some of that fund's investors. After all, many of them will have been actively solicited by the bank personnel in the first place. In short, at present there may be a lot of non-traditional money in equity mutual funds that has no business being there.

It is not uncommon for the bank to refer customers who want greater mutual fund selection to the bank's own full-service brokerage department. Brokers at the bank-owned firms will often try to establish a referral network with the bank managers to grow their own client base. In return they will try to refer loan or estate business back to the bank branches. At present, depending upon whom you speak to, this system appears to be reasonably successful for the participants. The broker gets a nice channel of new clients that takes very little work to develop (as opposed to the cold call method which can take a lot of time and energy) and the banker gets potential new loan or bank related business from these brokers. The big stumbling block in this relationship is the fact that the broker probably makes a great deal more money from this client-sharing arrangement than the branch manager. Therefore, at present, the banks are in the process of trying to find ways to even out the discrepancy so that every party involved will be more willing to share the client's business. As for the client, this process will appear to be advantageous, since he or she gets a direct referral from the bank manager to someone who is, in all probability, more knowledgeable about a broader range of investment products.

Another technique currently being used by some banks and their local branches is the practice of cross selling. (They all publicly deny this practice but it does happen.) A bank manager, when negotiating a mortgage with a client or prospective client, may offer a lower interest rate in return for the client transferring his or her RRSP account to the bank. In doing so, the branch may sacrifice a little income from the mortgage offered, but it gets all the RRSP business (which may include stock trading commissions, monies on GICs or bond purchases, and commissions, management fees or trailer fees, depending upon the mutual fund(s) purchased by the client).

The lower mortgage rate offered by the bank will certainly benefit the client. However, the client's relationship with his or her broker or financial institution may end because of the attractive carrot that the new bank is holding out. There is nothing wrong with healthy competition, but it is unfortunate that many good brokerage houses and brokers cannot compete in this situation because of the powers that have been given to the banks through favourable legislation changes in recent years. If the client switches the RRSP account and is happy, the result will of course be a net benefit to the client. If the switch does not work to the client's liking, however, the client will probably have lost more in terms of return, time, or peace of mind than he or she has gained from the lower mortgage rate. Any investor who is presented with this situation should research it thoroughly, and should ask a lot of questions in trying to determine if the offer is genuinely beneficial. The investor should even ask the bank manager why he can't give you the preferential mortgage rate in the first place. He probably can!

Trust Companies

Most trust companies provide similar services to those of the banks. Trust companies originally provided executor, trustee and registrar services. Today the differences between banks and trust companies are minimal. In fact, as far as the mutual fund purchaser is concerned, the differences are of no significance. Although trust companies haven't purchased major brokerage houses, they do emphasize their own in-house managed money products and will help the client invest money in this area. It is worth noting that the five big banks also own trust companies, which further adds to the banks' muscle in the Canadian financial marketplace.

Mutual Fund Companies

There are many companies today, both publicly and privately owned, that operate solely for the purpose of managing money on behalf of their clients. Mutual fund companies fall into this category as they often provide money management services to pension and trust funds, high net worth individuals and a variety of other clients. They also offer mutual funds that may be purchased by the general public. In general, mutual fund companies may be divided into two basic types:

- the no-load funds, that do their own marketing and advertising, and

- the companies that charge fees for purchases, and that tend to use independent brokerage firms, mutual fund dealers' sales forces, and financial planners, for distribution.

No-load funds have become increasingly popular in Canada, largely as a result of their performance numbers and the public exposure resulting from those numbers. It may also be argued that the public has become better informed about mutual funds because of the hot markets in recent years and the media attention that they have garnered. The no-load fund companies allow investors to invest directly with the company, which provides all of the other services (such as trustee and registrar services) in-house. Many of the no-load customers are generated through direct advertising, rather than through the efforts of an external sales force.

The commission funds (or "fee funds"), in contrast, do much of their sales through brokers, financial planners, or other independent networks. Until recently, many of the fee funds invested heavily in education and marketing for the sales network, often offering luxurious trips as incentive bonuses to those salespeople who achieved certain targets over the year. These conferences often have educational seminars so as to comply with the regulations set by the securities regulators. In addition to these conferences, there are marketing materials and advertising campaigns which brokers sometimes run together with a fund company (where the company pays most of the costs), all of which have increased the public exposure of these companies. While the companies still direct a lot of money towards sales networks, the recent Stromberg Report and the resulting industry Sales Practices Code has eliminated many of the conflict of interest issues from the fund company distribution relationship.

Unlike the no-load companies, fee fund companies will rarely take orders directly from the public, and will refer most inquiries to the independent salespeople who sell their funds. This of course makes sense for the fee fund companies because:

- they do not alienate their loyal sales force (if they *did* take orders directly and charged fees that were lower than brokers' fees, they would have very few brokers promoting their funds) and

- they rely on the salespeople to stay in complete compliance with the "know your client" rule.

Finally, although most fee fund companies don't employ their own sales force, there is a small minority that do (such as the Investors Group).

Independent Financial Planners

Although there are many independent financial planners that actively sell mutual funds, their profession has remained relatively unregulated. There are plans (in accordance with one of the recommendations in the recent Stromberg Report) to better regulate this sector, and some guidance is provided by a number of industry bodies such as the Association of Independent Financial Planners (AIFP) and the Canadian Association of Financial Planners (CAFP); nevertheless it is relatively easy to set up shop as a financial planner. Currently, there are two types of financial planners: those who provide a financial plan for a fee and those who actively sell the products that they recommend to clients (earning a commission on the product and in most cases earning a fee on the plan as well).

An investor may feel more comfortable dealing with a fees-only planner, knowing that the planner will not compromise his or her planning recommendations to earn fees by selling specific products. The investor should ascertain up-front whether or not the planner will earn commissions, so that the investor can decide whether he or she is comfortable with this arrangement. A great deal of trust is given to the planner in this scenario, and the client or investor would be well-advised to get references or a recommendation from someone who has used that particular planner with favourable results. In fairness, every salesperson (no matter where he or she works) should be subject to the same kind of scrutiny. Buyer beware.

Independently-Owned Financial Service Companies

There has been a sizeable increase in the number of independently-owned financial service companies that derive most of their revenue through the sale of mutual funds. If one looks closely on many city streets or at small town street intersections, there are quite a few walk-in store fronts that advertise mutual funds or fixed income rates. These proprietors have agreements in place to sell many of the larger fund company funds, and generally serve the smaller client. Often these proprietors have prior sales experience in insurance or mutual fund sales and find working for themselves either more enjoyable or profitable (or both).

Much of what a successful salesperson, financial planner or broker knows is often learned through experience and a lot of outside reading and research over many years. This cannot be taught in courses, despite the desires of the regulators of the industry to do so. So, a list of (perhaps very respectable) degrees beside an investment professional's name is no guarantee of investment success. One should still check references to determine the investment professional's product knowledge and ability to provide meaningful help. Once again, buyer beware.

Insurance Agents

While insurance salespeople generally make the lion's share of their fees from the sale of insurance products, they do offer mutual funds as a part of their product lines. The insurance industry is blessed with some very attractive investment products, largely as a result of the favourable tax treatment given to this sector. Without going into too much detail, products such as whole life insurance policies and prescribed annuities offer very attractive tax treatment to the investor who is trying to maximize return and minimize taxes. Unfortunately for many people, the life insurance industry has a bad name, largely as a result of the painful process that most income earning Canadians have faced when a friend or relative joins the industry and is actively encouraged to call everyone he or she knows and sell them life insurance policies. Despite that, these products can be a great benefit to many people. Unfortunately, I don't think many salespeople really understand the policies or can explain them very well. Having successfully completed the insurance licensing process, I noticed that very few of the salespeople who were brought in to speak at the in-house training seminar could adequately describe the products that they had been successfully selling for years. My own research has confirmed the benefits of these products, and I believe that they should be considered by most higher-net-worth working Canadians.

Many of the mutual funds offered by insurance companies differ in several ways from the more common open-end funds that most people buy today. Life insurance companies offer mutual fund-like products, known as segregated funds, which are technically insurance contracts. They guarantee the holder 75% of their capital back upon maturity date or death. The maturity date on these funds is usually ten years from the time of purchase. Many of the life insurance companies have boosted the guarantee to 100% on their segregated funds. This money back guarantee (which usually triggers after ten years, or upon the death of the holder[1]) can be an attractive feature to investors, but when examined closely, it really isn't as great a feature as it seems when you consider what inflation would do to $10,000 today and what that $10,000 would be worth ten years from now. Granted, if the equity markets did very poorly over the next ten years, or if a long period of deflation was experienced, these guarantees could prove to be very worthwhile.

Another very attractive feature of segregated funds is the fact that they are creditor-proof in many circumstances. For small business owners or lawyers in partnership arrangements, this is a wonderful benefit for personal savings. The fact that one's creditors can't seize the money in these types of investments gives licensed insurance salespeople a tremendous potential sales market with a product that is totally without competition. (Note: many lawyers or small business owners put all their personal assets in their spouse's name to avoid potential future loss through creditor action.

This can be a suitable solution for many; however for the unmarried, or for couples going through a divorce proceeding, problems may arise if assets have been unevenly distributed between the married individuals or not properly creditor-proofed by the unmarried person). It must also be mentioned that segregated funds avoid probate fees upon the death of the holder. Obviously, the benefit is that more money will go to the beneficiaries of the deceased if probate can be avoided.

Most segregated funds charge a fee if they are redeemed before a certain date (rear-end load) and have management fees or management expense ratios similar to open-end funds. Their performance can be followed through the daily net asset valuations found in most of the larger newspapers. Recently, many of Canada's larger insurance company sales forces have started selling mutual fund products offered by other mutual fund companies as a means of participating and profiting in the current mutual fund boom. (It should be noted here too, that independent fund companies with sales forces, such as Investors Group, have started doing the same thing.) This trend is in all probability beneficial to the investing public as there will undoubtedly be less pressure applied by the salesperson on the client to buy their own company's fund because the salesperson can, in most cases, receive the same commission from the sale of a competitor's product.

Because segregated funds are considered insurance contracts, their content is viewed as fully Canadian for RRSP purposes. The life insurance companies have been able to use this rule to their advantage, marketing segregated funds with high foreign content levels as 100% RRSP-eligible funds for those investors who want to load up on foreign holdings, yet stay within the 20% foreign content rule. Recently, the Finance Department stated that this situation will change in January, 1998, so as to "level out the playing field" for all mutual fund and segregated fund participants.

Finally, it should be mentioned that the insurance industry operates under its own regulatory organization with respect to its fund products, and sales practices may differ somewhat from the mutual fund industry which is regulated by the provincial securities administrations.

U.S. Mutual Funds

It is possible for Canadian citizens to buy mutual funds issued and sold in the U.S. The process is not easy, as different U.S. fund companies may have different rules regarding the purchase of their funds. Because the U.S. fund companies are not licensed to sell into Canada (some of the larger U.S. fund companies have Canadian subsidiaries and sell funds created specifically for Canadian investors) many companies will refuse to take orders directly from Canadian investors. Some fund companies may take orders if the investor can provide a U.S. address to which all materials relating to the fund purchase and maintenance can be sent. On the whole, this process is inconsistent and time consuming. For Canadians that want to own U.S.-issued funds, it is advisable to phone or write to the desired companies directly and inquire about their policy on non-resident purchases. Given the often lower management costs on U.S. equity funds, the added effort of acquiring some of these funds may well be worth it.

THE INVESTMENT FUNDS INSTITUTE OF CANADA

Total Assets by
Manager Member Type
March 1997

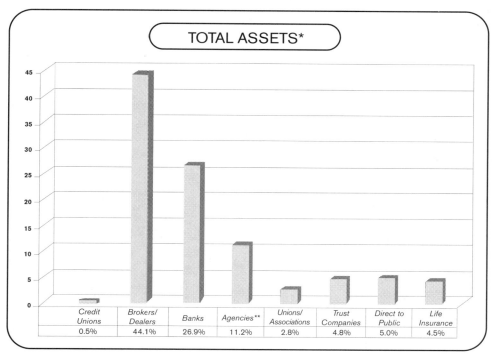

TOTAL ASSETS*

Credit Unions	Brokers/ Dealers	Banks	Agencies**	Unions/ Associations	Trust Companies	Direct to Public	Life Insurance
0.5%	44.1%	26.9%	11.2%	2.8%	4.8%	5.0%	4.5%

*Including Money Markets
** Fund companies that manage money and have their own sales force.

Key Points

- There are **many different companies** that sell and distribute mutual funds.

- Certain organizations or dealers may emphasize or promote specific mutual funds that are in their own interest. You should **be aware** of this practice when making the determination as to whether a fund is also in your best interest.

- There are both **commission** (or "fee") funds and **no-load** funds. They are, in many cases, marketed differently.

- Make sure you **understand** the **compensation arrangement** of your financial planner or investment advisor. They may charge a **fee only** for their planning work, or they may also receive **commission-type** fees for the funds that they recommend and sell.

- The insurance industry offers mutual funds (**segregated funds**) which have slightly different terms than traditional mutual funds and are regulated by a different governing body. There are some significant **benefits** to owning segregated funds.

- In certain cases, Canadian investors can buy **U.S. mutual funds**. The U.S. has a much greater number of funds available which, in general, have **lower management fees** than Canadian funds.

Notes:

[1] This feature can be a tremendous benefit, if it's included in estate planning.

Chapter 6

Understanding Prospectuses and Mutual Fund Investment Styles

The prospectus is a very important document that reveals many particulars about the fund company, the funds it manages, the investment styles and philosophies of the managers, and all fees and commissions involved in the investing process. Recently, in following the recommendations made by the Stromberg Report, a real attempt has been made by many fund companies to produce documents that are easy to read and understand. It still remains the role of the investor, however, to look closely at the fine print and try to thoroughly understand what he or she is investing in, and how it will be managed. Below is an explanation of the different investing styles that you may encounter in a mutual fund's prospectus.

Investment Styles

Money Market Funds

Generally, money market funds are managed to maximize income while preserving capital and maintaining liquidity. Money market funds must invest in products with maturities of one year or less, so there really isn't too much strategy or skill needed to manage this type of fund (although some money market managers may argue this point). For the same reason, most money market funds have similar performance records. Management fees and commission structures have a large part to play in final returns to investors with this kind of product, as some funds have higher fees than others. When buying or trying to decide among a number of money market funds, the investor should refer to the summary of fees and expenses set out at the front of each fund's simplified prospectus.

Bond Funds

Bond funds often have similar investment objectives to money market funds, but unlike money market funds they can often invest in bonds that have a duration of thirty years or longer. A bond fund manager in many cases will need to try to predict which way interest rates are heading, and will adopt a strategy to attempt to maximize the fund's rate of return through buying bonds of a specific duration. For example, if the manager feels long-term interest rates are going to fall, he or she will buy bonds of a long duration. Even a small drop in longer term interest rates can have a tremendous affect on the price of a bond.

Consider a bond with a maturity of twenty years at par, which is issued today with a coupon of 7%. The bond will yield 7% over the twenty years. If long-term interest rates drop one full percentage point the very next day down to 6% in the twenty year range, the bond would rise from a price of 100 (par) to approximately 113.84 (see the chart below). (This may be an extreme example, but it clearly illustrates the point.) Thus, if the bond was sold, the fund would make a 13.84% capital gain on the bond. Conversely, if interest rates rise one full percentage point to 8%, the bond would then be approximately worth $88.69.

The above example illustrates the potential volatility of holding a longer-term bond. It is the fund manager's responsibility to try to achieve the best possible rate of return, but, being human, the manager can of course be wrong sometimes. In 1994, for example, interest rates rose sharply with little warning, with the result that many bond funds had a negative rate of return for the year, since many of them had invested in bonds of longer maturities.

For the individual investor, sometimes it is easier just to buy the bonds directly and hold them to maturity. This eliminates the potential ups and downs of a bond fund's value and gives the investor the peace of mind that comes with knowing what will be earned on the bond's maturity. Bond funds are perpetual and do not have a maturity. The investor must weigh the benefits of each. (Derivatives may also be used at times for certain purposes in a fund, which will be indicated in the fund's prospectus.)

Government bonds, which formerly traded in units of $100, currently trade in units of $1000. The industry still quotes prices per $100 bond. For example, if a 10-year bond was purchased in June, 1997 and matures in 2007, and the market interest rates were 7%, that bond would trade at par or $100. If market interest rates went up to 9%, that $100 bond could be sold for $86.99. Conversely, if rates went down to 5%, then the $100 bond could be sold for $115.59.

Hypothetical Bond Scenario
Semi-Annual
No Change to Credit Quality
June 1 Settlement and Maturity

		5%	6%	7%	8%	9%	10%
7%*	June 1/00	105.51	102.71	100	97.38	94.84	92.38
7%*	June 1/02	108.12	103.96	100	96.21	92.59	89.14
7%*	June 1/07	115.59	107.44	100	93.20	86.99	81.31
7%*	June 1/27	130.91	113.84	100	88.69	79.36	71.61

* Coupon

The above table shows what a 1% movement (up or down) in interest rates (on the same day) does to the price of 3-, 5-, 10- and 30-year bonds at par with a 7% coupon.

Managing a foreign bond fund would be very similar to managing a domestic fund except that the fund manager's role includes buying bonds issued in foreign currencies to profit not only from interest rate changes but also currency appreciation. Foreign currency fluctuations play a significant role in how well a fund will perform in its domestic currency. In many instances, the currency will have a much greater effect on performance numbers than the bond prices and interest coupons. As a result, foreign bond funds are often much more volatile than domestic bond funds.

According to the *Bell Charts* there are two types of bond management styles.

Interest Rate Anticipation

This is the process of analysing and forecasting the trend of interest rates and then establishing an average term to maturity for the bond portfolio which will maximize the return (if the forecast is correct). Managers who engage in this process often use government bonds and thus do not have to concern themselves with credit quality ratings. The management style is usually to buy and hold bonds until certain targets are met.

Spread Trading

This is the process of switching from one bond to another to take advantage of anomalies that occur from time to time in the market place. The objective of spread trading is to improve the portfolio yield without increasing the risk level, or to decrease the risk level without reducing the yield. In this form of trading there is typically a lot more trading activity, and the manager must keep a vigilant eye on the yield curve. (The yield curve is a representation of the relationship between the yields of bonds of the same quality, but with different maturities.)

Equity Funds

For equity funds, there are several different styles or approaches that a fund manager may take in investing monies within a fund. Quite often, these are not clearly pointed out. For example, a common investment objective that appears in prospectus after prospectus is "to achieve long-term growth of capital". What does this mean, and how does the fund manager go about doing it? Talk about diversification usually includes a mention of investing in different asset classes (e.g. real estate, common stocks, bonds etc.). It is, however, very important that one also diversifies in different management styles when investing in equity funds. The different styles of management will be variously suited to certain phases in the market, as we shall see.

Below are listed several styles or philosophies used in managing equity mutual funds.

Value Investing

As defined by the *Bell Charts*, "Value investors seek to invest in companies at a price which is low relative to the intrinsic value of the company and to the valuation that the market has placed on similar companies." The approach is to acquire assets at bargain basement prices and sell them when the valuation levels rise.

Value investing generally focuses on stocks that trade with above-average yields while trading at below-average price earnings multiples. One of the best books subscribing to this particular investment style is Benjamin Graham's *The Intelligent Investor*. In fact, Warren Buffett, one of America's richest men (and considered an icon in the investment business) has touted it as the best book ever written about investing. Value investors try to find companies that are considerably undervalued by the market. These companies will have certain assets that are overlooked, such as trademarks, or rights or privileges, that often don't show up on balance sheets, or perhaps real estate that does show up on the balance sheet, but at an undervalued figure. Undervalued assets such as these, coupled with good management, should eventually bring a company to be fairly priced by the market. Only when the market prices the stock fairly (in the opinion of the fund manager or the investor) will the value investor sell the stock. It is important to note that in the current market environment it is very difficult to find even a few undervalued stocks that fit these criteria in terms of price earnings multiples and dividend yields. Therefore, some managers have to adapt or modify how they define value. This is where fund managers who use the value investment style can get into trouble, since they have to be fully invested most of the time, even when true value may be nearly impossible to find.

Growth Investing

Growth investing seeks long-term capital appreciation with dividend income being more or less incidental[1]. The objective is to find companies with strong growth in sales and earnings. Through continued earnings growth, the investor can receive above-average stock price appreciation. By their very nature, growth stocks tend to be a little more volatile than the traditional "blue chip" or established companies that operate in more mature markets or industries. Interestingly though, many of the traditional Dow Jones Industrial 30 stocks are companies that operate in mature markets but are currently trading with growth stock multiples, possibly because of the political and economic changes that have occurred throughout the world over the past six to seven years. With the break up of the former Soviet Union and the move towards capitalism in China and the Far East, many companies long thought of as having limited or mature markets (e.g. Coca Cola and the tobacco companies) now have, or are perceived to have, excellent earnings growth potential by moving into these new markets. This situation however should be treated with caution.

Peter Lynch, who managed the Fidelity Magellan fund, gained a measure of fame as a growth fund manager. Lynch amassed tremendous returns by buying into a large number of companies (his portfolio usually contained hundreds of companies) that fit the growth criteria. His belief was that if one, or maybe even two, stocks out of ten performed well (by going up ten-fold) he would be more than happy. The nature of capitalism is that most companies will fail, but if a fund manager can from time to time catch the ones that do succeed, the fund will achieve superior results. Growth fund managers will often ignore general economic conditions because growth companies will be around in both good times and and bad, and their shareholders will eventually be rewarded through price appreciation based on increased earnings.

It is very important to note that mutual fund managers (and investors in general) will often invest in companies that show growth *potential,* despite not having any current revenues or earnings. The stock price of a company can often rise significantly before there are any real revenues or sales. It is at this point that the investment risk can be greatest for the investor. Companies that trade on stock exchanges know that what the "street" is often looking for in companies is good growth potential. It is quite normal for a company to put an optimistic outlook on its future prospects in spite of the reality of a more modest, or even mediocre, future potential. Companies may in fact hire outside public relations firms (or promoters) to promote the company to money managers. In return, the company might pay the PR firms in the form of stock options. The higher the stock price goes, the more the PR firm makes. Furthermore, many companies use stock options as a reward for good management performance. If the stock price rises, the managers can make a lot more money on these options than from their regular salaries. There is nothing wrong with this process if the company realistically believes that the targets it has set are obtainable. In some instances, however, there may be very little, if any, truth to the rosy scenario being circulated. It is much safer to buy into "growth" companies *after* real earnings are achieved (although very few start-up companies ever get to this stage). After a company establishes an earnings track record there is usually still tremendous upside potential for the stock price and investors can make great gains even if they weren't in right from the start.

Along this line, companies sometimes use very liberal forms of accounting which can create the appearance of growing earnings when in fact the exact opposite may be occurring. For example, it is possible for companies to include many expenses (items that should be deducted against income) on the balance sheet as assets, thus artificially increasing the reported earnings. When a closer inspection of the financial statements is made public, or when the long-term effects of this practice are realized (often involving a huge write-down for the company) the stock price of the company usually tumbles, leaving many shareholders that much poorer. Conversely, the fund manager who can ride these questionable companies on the upswing, can in some instances get a lot of money out before the slide occurs, thus enhancing shareholders' returns in spite of the tremendous risk.

The above-mentioned scenario illustrates how the investment game may be played at certain times by certain companies and individuals. There are instances, as mentioned earlier, of a company reporting a consistent increase in profits quarter after quarter and then, in the very next quarter, filing for Chapter 11 (bankruptcy) protection. Money and fund managers are not immune to this, when they have been lied to, been naive or failed to do adequate homework. And in a strong bull market, there always seem to be more and more "great" companies with "great" prospects landing on fund managers' laps. In times like these, the mutual fund investor needs a reliable and disciplined fund manager.

Momentum Investing

In recent times "momentum investing" has become a popular management style, primarily among some U.S. fund managers. Momentum investing (much like technical analysis) involves studying the price movements and the volume of stock traded with respect to the desired companies, in an attempt to achieve investment gains. The simple rule of thumb is to buy stocks that are going up on large volume. In his 1991 book entitled *Successful Stock Market Speculation*, Ted Carter points out that you don't necessarily have to know much about the company — the volumes and price increases can sometimes tell you all you need to know (i.e., "Somebody knows something and you had better get in").

By studying price and volume charts, momentum players will often get in and out of stocks much more quickly than value or growth managers, and will basically try to "ride the wave" on the upside. I spoke with an offshore fund manager who used this method in purchasing a biotechnology stock that had no earnings (and no immediate prospects of earnings) but that was trading at a ridiculously high market capitalization. He achieved a rate of return of over 70% in a period of months, despite having very little idea about what the company did. Despite success stories such as the above, momentum investing will often result in losses when the charts and the momentum don't go as planned.

Momentum investing requires strict discipline. Momentum investors will often set "stops" underneath the stock price, which means that a stock will automatically be sold if it drops below the "stop" level. The theory is that the small losses that will inevitably occur will pale in comparison to the huge gains made by catching the big movers.

This strategy can backfire if the stock is halted on a stock exchange (because of bad news or unfavourable announcements) and then opens below the "stop" price. In this case the investor can't get out at the desired price. Bre-X is a good example: the stock was halted in the high teens, and subsequently opened at $2.50.

Finally, the frequency of trades in this management style means that it will often have much higher costs (i.e., commissions) that can eat into investment gains, and the gains achieved are "realized" meaning that more taxes are paid more often.

Other Equity Fund Investment Styles

A fund manager will generally have his or her own investment style or philosophy, which may incorporate a combination of any of the above three management styles. It is well known throughout the investment industry that certain investment styles do better in certain kinds of markets. Most importantly, no one can know which style will be most rewarded by the market at the time. As a result, funds of funds or investment packages which incorporate various managers with different styles have become popular, as a way of reducing overall portfolio volatility.

The names and descriptions of the various investment styles may differ somewhat in various prospectuses. Despite this variation, the actual styles will in many cases be very similar to the three styles mentioned above. Some of the more common variations are described below.

Blend

An investment style that can use a number of different approaches to portfolio management (e.g. growth, value etc.).

Top Down

This management style seeks to analyse the economy and equity markets first, before making the decision to purchase stocks. The manager will often decide on a certain country or group of markets as most attractive, and will then purchase equities in those areas. Less analysis is given to the specific stocks or companies in which the fund is investing. In fact, the fund manager may simply buy index funds in the desired market(s). Top down investing may be combined with bottom up investing.

Bottom Up

This investment approach looks exclusively for companies that meet the manager's investment criteria, with very little concern for the market or economic conditions. Cash will usually be held until a suitable company is found.

Sector Investing

This management style seeks out the sectors of the economy (e.g. real estate, hi-tech etc.) that will perform well, or will experience the greatest growth potential in the short term. The philosophy behind sector investing is the belief that areas of future growth can successfully be anticipated, and that exceptional profit growth can be realized from good companies in these areas before the rest of the market catches on. This approach can incorporate many investment criteria for choosing which companies to buy after the desired market area has been identified.

Sector investing funds often have greater volatility than other, more diversified, equity funds, because of their heavy concentration in one area. There are both pros and cons to this approach.

Investors should be aware that some funds can quickly become sector-like in their investment holdings, despite the fact that there may be no specific mention of concentration on one sector in the prospectus. For example, in recent years, a fund company operating in Canada offered a U.S. equity fund that had a very good performance record over a period of time. Although the defined objectives (i.e., growth etc.) were clearly stated in the prospectus, closer examination of the fund's holdings revealed that the fund was highly concentrated in one area (in this case, airline stocks). As a result of the great initial performance of the fund, the asset size of the fund ballooned because of the influx of money from new investors trying to capitalize on the fund's great track record. Unfortunately, the investments that the fund manager moved into next did not perform as well as many had expected, and the manager was relegated to mere mortal status. This consistent heavy weighting in one specific sector was not mentioned in the prospectus and the fund's previous great performance was not attributed to the "sector investing" management style. The investors were thus exposed to both the benefits and the risks inherent in sector investing.

Another interesting story involved a newly-created mutual fund company in Canada that brought in a top-performing money manager from the U.S. to manage its U.S. equity fund. While the objective of the fund was growth, again there was no mention of sector investing in the prospectus. This particular manager, however, had made tremendous gains in the cable and cellular telephone sector and had achieved spectacular gains on the backs of top stocks in that sector. The fund was an early hit with investors, who expected to make big gains with a top manager. However, the fund manager continued to purchase stocks in that sector even as the prices started to come off. The fund manager, it appeared, had become married to these companies. In fact, when a particular company that was held by the fund made an announcement, the press, in commenting on the release, quoted the fund manager as a spokesperson for the company. It was also rumoured that the fund was helping make a market on the stocks that it held. (The term "making a market" means that the fund, or fund manager, helps support the stock price when sellers appear in the market.) Needless to say, the fund severely under-performed most mutual funds over this period and the fund manager was soon let go.

As revealed by these stories, great returns on funds can in some cases be the result of heavy weighting in one or two sectors. Quite often these excellent returns are hard to repeat on a long-term basis. It is advisable, therefore, to check the fund's investments to ensure that it is well diversified. There is nothing wrong with a fund being concentrated in a certain sector, as long as the prospectus is clear about it, and as long as the investor knows that the fund may be more volatile as a consequence.

It is usually prudent for the fund buyer to examine the current or most recent portfolio holdings of the desired fund and to discuss his or her concerns with a broker or the fund's representative. This will give the buyer a clearer understanding of the type of fund into which he or she is buying. It will help the investor to better understand how and why the fund is performing the way it is and to set realistic expectations as to the fund's future performance. Furthermore, the fund buyer will be better able to diversify through purchasing other funds with different management styles.

Sector funds and income trusts investing in specific sectors (e.g. oil and gas and real estate) have become very popular lately. Investors must keep in mind, when buying these kinds of products, that the heavy weighting in a specific area could result in volatility, despite the attractive yields or returns that many of these products (particularly income trusts) are currently paying. Of particular interest is a sector fund that invests specifically in publicly-traded financial service companies. This fund has had an incredible return over the past ten years. Many of the companies held in the fund have had exponential earnings growth, largely as a result of the huge increase in the volume of money flowing into mutual funds since the beginning of the 1990s. If the market turns, this fund could drop much faster than almost any of the other funds in the market. (Interestingly, this particular fund dropped 30% during the crash of 1987, and I would venture a guess that few of today's holders of this fund know this, or were invested in the fund at the time of the crash.)

Key Points

- It is important to **read the prospectus** of a mutual fund carefully, as it tells the investor **how the fund will be managed.**

- The **two basic management styles** for bond funds are **interest rate anticipation** and **spread trading.**

- There are **many different management styles** for equity funds and the buyer should be aware of **which strategy** (or combination of strategies) will be used.

- It may be a good idea to **diversify over a number of management styles** as the market will **reward different styles** at **different times** (with little or no predictability).

- Although **momentum investing** is currently a popular management style (with rising equity prices) it should be approached with **extreme caution**. Even a **small market correction** can have an incredibly **negative effect** on momentum type stocks.

Notes:

[1] John C. Bogle, *Bogle on Mutual Funds*, p. 67. New York: Dell Publishing.

Chapter 7

Mutual Fund Sales Charges and Fees

There are many different fees associated with the purchasing, holding and selling of mutual funds that most investors are unaware of. It is very important to understand the fee structures of the funds that you buy. They can have a tremendous impact on your investment returns. In general, equity funds usually have higher acquisition fees than bond funds and money market funds. (In fact, some bond funds and money market funds have no acquisition costs at all.)

The first kind of fee is the sales charge. This is the commission that is paid to the broker or distributor upon purchase or redemption of the fund. There are three different kinds of sales charges:

1. a regular "front-end" sales charge
   ("front-end load" or "up-front" charge)

2. a deferred or "back-end" sales charge, and

3. "no-load" (i.e. no sales charge)

Front-End Sales Charge

This fee is taken at the time of purchase and is usually given as a percentage. For example if $100 of a given fund is purchased, and the front-end or up-front charge is 5%, the dealer receives a $5 sales commission, and the investor will begin with $95 invested. In previous years, the industry in Canada was able to charge up to 9%, but this number has come down recently and is generally in the 4% to 6% range now. Investors should understand that this rate is often negotiable and can be lowered upon agreement with the sales representative. The mutual fund industry is currently so competitive that some discount houses are now offering some of the "big name" funds at around 2%. It is important to note here that the track records that are posted in the financial press do not take into consideration the front-end load fee, so almost invariably a fund's reported performance differs from the actual return received by the investor on a front-end load fund in the first year. (The front-end load is a one-time charge.)

Back-End Load Sales Charge

Unlike the front-end sales structure, mutual funds purchased under the back-end or deferred sales charge method do not levy a sales charge at the time of purchase, but require payment of a commission on the redemption of the mutual fund. Quite often the commission charged is on a declining scale. For example, if the investor cashes out of the fund in the first year, he or she might pay a charge of 6% of the total value of the shares at the time. The fee will decline gradually for subsequent years, and if the fund is held long enough (usually anywhere between five and nine years) it can be possible to pay no fees at all.

It is worth noting that each mutual fund company has its own back-end fee structure. There are many variations in these back-end fee structures. For example, some fund companies charge a back-end fee based on the initial amount invested. For example, a $10,000 initial investment would be charged 3% (or $300) for cashing out of the fund at the end of five years. Another company may have the same 3% redemption charge after 5 years, but it may be based on the value of the fund at the time of redemption instead of the initial investment. In this case, the initial $10,000 investment may be worth $15,000 and the charge would be $450 (3% of $15,000). Not all fund companies offer this option so it is important to find out before purchasing a certain fund if this option is available (or desirable). Given the choice, most investors would rather not pay any acquisition charges at all, so for the investor who plans on buying and holding, or who plans to stay with the same family of funds (there are usually no fees for switching between funds managed by the same fund company) this can often be a better option than the front-end commission.

Back-end load fee structures became popular in the latter half of the 1980s when the first mutual fund limited partnership was created. It was generally believed by people in the brokerage and mutual fund industry that brokers would find it easier to sell funds if the client didn't have to pay a fee up-front. Instead of the broker receiving a commission from the client, the limited partnership would pay the broker the commission and then share in the management fees of the funds that were sold under this arrangement. The limited partnership would also collect any and all of the back-end commissions charged to clients cashing out of the funds. The brokers were happy because the funds were easier to sell, and the fund companies were happy because the clients were more inclined to stay with the fund company until they could cash in with no back-end charge (again, anywhere from 5 to 9 years). The limited partnership holders were also happy because they got a nice tax write-off and a healthy income stream from sharing the management fees with the fund company (usually 0.5% per annum) and the redemption fees (some starting as high as 6% in the first year).

Example of Redemption Charges for a Fund Family

IF REDEEMED DURING THE FOLLOWING PERIODS AFTER DATE OF ISSUE	REDEMPTION CHARGES AS A PERCENTAGE OF AMOUNT REDEEMED		
	MORTGAGE FUND	BOND FUND	ALL OTHER FUNDS
1st year	3.3%	4.4%	5.5%
2nd year	3.3%	4.4%	5.5%
3rd year	2.7%	3.6%	4.5%
4th year	2.4%	3.2%	4.0%
5th year	2.1%	2.8%	3.5%
6th year	1.5%	2.0%	2.5%
7th year	0.9%	1.2%	1.5%
thereafter	Nil	Nil	Nil

Table shows redemption charges which may apply if redemption charge securities are redeemed within the stated time periods after purchase (if investor's purchase is under the Redemption Charge Option.)

An important point regarding back-end load funds is that there may be a higher management expense ratio for choosing the back-end load option. The reason behind this higher fee is that part of the fees earned by the fund manager must go towards paying the limited partners or the fund company itself who finance the commissions to the broker when this option is chosen. As a result, this additional fee (usually around 0.5% annually) goes to the financier, and is often indirectly paid by the fundholder. So, in essence, the fundholder should consider this option carefully, as it may be better to pay a 2 to 3% fee up front rather than paying an additional 0.5% for each year that the fund is held. In other cases, the broker who sells the back-end load fund will receive 0.5% less per annum in trailer fees, in which case the investor would pay the same fees as under a front-end load option. Anyone buying back-end load funds should ask what the fees are under both options.

Finally, under the back-end fee structure, many funds allow purchasers to take up to 10% of their investment out of the fund annually with no charge. Again, it is important to find out if this added feature is available before buying the fund.

No-Load Fee Structure

No-load funds charge neither a front-end nor a back-end fee upon acquisition or disposal of the fund. They are usually offered by banks, trust companies or private fund companies (Altamira is a good example in Canada). These funds are often marketed through newspapers and television ads, since no external sales force is used. The companies offering these funds are content to earn their money through the management fees that they charge. It is important to note that these kinds of funds can usually be bought through brokers, so it is often possible to hold these funds at one place and in one account, as opposed to having to go to each fund company separately to invest in the particular funds desired. However, brokers won't solicit orders for no-load funds, since they don't generally receive a commission on the sale.

Management Expense Ratio (MER)

After looking at the sales charges of a mutual fund, it is also very important to consider the management expense ratio of the fund. There are three primary component fees that make up a mutual fund's expense ratio. They are:

- Management fees (including trailer fees)
- Administrative costs
- Other operating expenses

In the U.S. there is an additional component of MER known as the 12b-1 distribution fee.

These fees generally make up the largest cost that a fund holder will incur in owning mutual funds because they are charged to the fund on an annual basis, and are deducted from the fund's assets before performance is calculated. They are automatically (and quite probably "invisibly") deducted from the fund value, usually on a monthly basis. The chart below shows the MERs for a typical family of funds.

MERs for a Typical Family of Funds

	MGMT. FEE (%)	EXPENSE RATIO (%)
Americas Fund	2.00	2.45
Canadian Growth Fund Limited	2.00	2.43
Canadian Resource Fund	2.00	2.43
European Opportunities Fund	2.00	2.58[1]
Far East Fund	2.00	2.56
Growth Fund	2.00	2.35[1]
Japan Fund	2.00	2.58
U.S. Emerging Growth Fund	2.00	2.46
U.S. Money Market Fund	1.00	2.25[1]
World Asset Allocation Fund	2.00	2.45
World Balanced RRSP Fund	2.00	2.43
World Emerging Growth Fund	2.00	2.55
World Equity Fund	2.00	2.46
World Growth RRSP Fund	2.00	2.46[1]
World Income RRSP Fund	1.75	2.21[2]
World Precious Metals Fund	2.00	2.56

[1] annualized rate for new fund.
[2] annualized rate applying higher management fee rate in effect since September 16, 1994.

Management Fees

This is the fee paid to the fund manager for supervision and portfolio implementation on behalf of the fundholders. The fees for equity funds in the U.S. range from around 0.5% to 1.5% per annum and are slightly lower for bond funds and money market funds. In Canada the management fees tend to be higher: between 1.75% and 2.5% for equities, from 1% to 1.5% for bond funds and around 0.5% for money market funds. Why fees are higher in Canada is a good question. Ellen Roseman of the *Globe and Mail* wrote an interesting article recently comparing the different MERs between Canada and the U.S. The chart below shows the different MERs for all fund types.

Fund expenses, Canada vs. U.S.
Asset-weighted management-expense ratios (MERs), March '96

	Canada	U.S.	Canada/U.S. Relative Gap (%)
Long-term funds	**2.06%**	**1.27%**	**62%**
All equity funds	2.13	1.51	41
Canadian equity funds	2.14	n/a	n/a
U.S. equity funds	2.23	1.42	57
International equity funds	2.27	1.82	24
Balanced funds	1.91	1.40	36
All bond funds	1.52	1.02	49
Tax-exempt bond funds	–	0.93	–
Other bond funds	1.52	1.12	35

Source: Investor Economics Insight

From: *"Why Canadian Investors pay more,"* Ellen Roseman, *The Globe and Mail*, Wednesday, October 23, 1996, p. B17.

Roseman states that the Investment Funds Institute of Canada claims that the cost differential between Canadian and U.S. MERs is 0.25% to 0.3% on average, but that the statistics don't reflect this estimate. Earl Bederman, president of Investor Economics, has studied the topic and gives some possible explanations for this difference. His study reveals a 0.79% differential between Canadian and U.S. mutual fund fees (on average) and cites the following reasons:

1. Product mix: Canada on average has a greater proportion of equity funds, which almost always cost more to manage than money market and bond funds.

2. Sales charges (in this case the cost of marketing) are reflected in the MER in Canada whereas U.S. sales charges are likely to be kept separate from the fees and expenses charged to the fund. (The 12b-1 numbers have been factored into the preceding graph—see "The 12b-1 Distribution Fee," below.)

3. Economies of scale: U.S. equity funds tend to be nine times the size of Canadian equity funds (this category had the largest fee differential, being 0.81% higher for Canadian funds).

Other smaller factors often cited are that Canadian mutual fund material must be printed in two languages, and that Canada has ten different securities regulators that require separate filings (as compared with one in the U.S.).

This cost differential in fees charged on funds is significant and it is worth reiterating here that Canadians can buy U.S. mutual funds (see Chapter 5). As we shall see, management fees can be a large drag on longer-term rates of return.

Trailer Fees

Another component of the management fee is a trailer commission paid by the fund's manager to the broker or dealer who sold the fund. The trailer fee is an incentive for the broker, who is usually paid quarterly, to keep the client in the fund and to provide continuing advice and service. The trailer fee is usually anywhere from 0.25% to as much as 1.5% per annum, depending on what kind of fund is chosen. Bond and money market funds tend to be on the lower side while equity funds usually charge higher trailers.

The recent Stromberg Report (see Appendix A) recommended that trailer fees be terminated voluntarily by the industry, but if they continued, that they be paid on the first asset sold by the broker (i.e., a $10,000 sale would generate $25 annually for a broker if the trailer fee was 0.25%). Until recently, the industry only started paying trailer fees after $100,000 had been sold in one fund family group, citing the costs of implementation on smaller sales. The Stromberg report wants to eliminate all biases so that a broker will not just sell one or two fund families so as to reach the trailer fee minimum (which could also be a potential conflict of interest). This recommendation has recently been implemented. It is worth noting that many no-load funds will pay a trailer fee to brokers who place orders in these funds. This means that even if the broker or salesperson doesn't recommend the fund to the client, he or she will gladly place the order anyway, in order to receive the trailer fee. Some no-load funds pay no trailer fees at all; as a result they can have MERs that are considerably lower than the no-load funds that *do* have trailer fees.

Some mutual funds also have incentive and penalty fees, so that good performance (as measured by percentage gain or as compared to a given index) may pay the fund manager a greater fee, while poor performance may result in the reduction of fees. These fees are usually highlighted in the prospectus and their intentions are clear and fair.

Administrative Costs

These costs are related to the everyday functioning of the fund, i.e. record-keeping, transaction services and general administrative services provided to the fund. Quite often, the payment of these costs will be made directly to the fund's adviser, as the fund company will provide these services in-house. These fees can range from 0.2% to 0.4% of the fund's average assets per annum.

Other Operating Expenses

These include costs incurred by the fund itself such as custodial fees, taxes, legal and audit expenses and directors' fees[1]. They can run from 0.1% to 0.3% of the fund's assets per annum. In the U.S., some fund companies will include brokerage commissions for transactions as part of this expense in their prospectuses. In Canada, National Policy 39 excludes brokerage commissions and taxes from the MER. This is a very interesting area because it can frequently be impossible to estimate the costs of brokerage from year to year. In his book, *Bogle On Mutual Funds*, John Bogle refers to this as the "invisible cost," and cites studies that put this cost at 0.5% to 2% per year.

Depending on the size of the fund and the turnover rate of the portfolio (i.e. the number of transactions in the portfolio) these costs can have a very large impact on the fund's performance. The smaller the fund, the greater the fees in percentage terms. The more trading activity, the greater the dollar value of commissions paid. In addition, there are the costs of carrying out transactions through the bid/ask spread. Finally, there are the "market impact" costs, which essentially means that buying tends to push the price of the stock up and selling tends to push the stock price down. All these things put a drag on fund performance.

The 12b-1 Distribution Fee

The 12b-1 distribution fee (an American term) allows funds to charge fund shareholders a fee which in essence is used to help pay the costs of marketing, advertising and distributing a fund. In some cases it also helps to pay commissions to sales representatives[2]. The rationale given for this fee is that it helps the fund grow in size, which helps reduce the fund's costs through greater economies of scale. Another way of looking at it, is that it is a way in which funds can charge existing shareholders to help bring in more assets on which to charge a fee. Depending on how you look at it, currently 60% of equity mutual funds in the U.S. charge a 12b-1 fee, which can lead to a higher overall cost and which results in an average "expense ratio" of 1.51% for all equity funds. (Again, the numbers vary based on the way the numbers are calculated.)

U.S. Equity Fund Expense Ratios *(1961–92)*

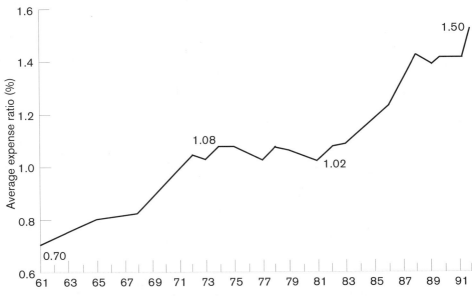

Source: John Bogle, *Bogle on Mutual Funds*, p. 203.

The average expense ratio for Canadian equity funds is 2.13%. (Again, the numbers vary slightly based on calculation differences.) While the 12b-1 fee does not exist in Canada, Canadian fund companies do use some of the money from the management fees to market their products. A look through fund prospectuses will show that many fund companies pay for advertising themselves (regulations insist on this). Dealers who will "joint market" by highlighting a fund company's product will often be helped by that fund company.

Things to Think About

From the graph on the previous page, it is clear that fees in the U.S. for managing money on behalf of others have increased at a very healthy rate. For Canadian investors, the average MER averages around 2.13% for equity funds, which is clearly much higher than the (U.S.) expense ratios depicted on the graph, above. In an industry that has supposedly become more competitive, it appears that fees have risen consistently. In fact, according to Gordon Powers (*Globe and Mail*, May 10, 1997, p. B20), MERs for equity funds in Canada have risen from 1.81% in 1990 to 2.21% in 1996. There are several interesting explanations as to how and why this has happened.

A request for a fee hike must be approved by the fund's directors. They are elected by the fund's shareholders to (at least in theory) look out for the shareholders' best interests. In many cases, a fund's directors are nominated by, or friendly with, the fund company itself and may not necessarily be as objective as one would hope. As a way of putting the fee hike in perspective, fund directors will often compare the fee hike with other fund companies' fees. Essentially this has caused an upward spiral in fees.

These fee hikes may seem unfair given the huge profits that fund managers make in managing other people's money. They are not completely unfair, however, because the fund investors have a choice in this matter: they can "vote with their feet" (or perhaps, one should say, their money). Investors can reject the request for a fee increase, or they can simply cash in their fund and look elsewhere. Unfortunately, most people don't have the time to do the sort of homework necessary to stay on top of all these issues. It is, however, imperative to understand as much as possible about mutual funds if you wish to invest in them. Ultimately that is the only way to ensure that your best interests are being served.

Mutual Fund Sales Charges and Fees

Ruth Simon, in the February, 1995 edition of *The Money Ranking*, did an extensive study of the fee structures of mutual funds and their trends over recent times. Here are some of the highlights of the analysis:

- Mutual fund investors pay nearly twice as much as institutional investors for money management.

- U.S. diversified stock funds have jacked up their annual fees nearly 35% over the past 16 years.

- There are potential conflict of interest situations where fund managers perform the fund's brokerage transactions with brokerage firms that they partly own. (This situation is usually restricted in Canada, and filing is usually required with regulators.)

Simon also presents data which clearly shows the drag that large expense ratios play on returns.

In another study presented in the same article, *Morningstar* analysed U.S. equity funds over a ten-year period ending on November 30th, 1995. Their research revealed that funds with expense ratios under 1.36% returned an average of 13.1% annually over this period. Funds with expense ratios above 1.36% yielded only 11.1%. Other studies done by the Securities and Exchange Commission (SEC) and Princeton University indicate that from 1971 to 1993, for every percentage point a typical equity fund spent on expenses, its return dropped 1.9%.

The odds clearly favour those funds with lower expense ratios. The question of fees ultimately leads to the discussion of bypassing money managers altogether and investing in the index funds where the funds simply mimic the stock index chosen (see Chapter 15). In fact, in 1996 only 25% of the available equity mutual funds outperformed the S&P 500 index. In 1995 that number was only 16% (U.S. figures).

I recently spoke with Harold Hands, Chairman of the Board of the Investment Funds Institute of Canada, regarding the trend in management expense ratios in Canada and the differences in MERs between Canadian and U.S. mutual funds. Mr. Hands states that MERs have declined since the early 1990s in many parts of the industry as a result of the strong growth in assets by the industry. These statements are clearly in stark contrast to Gordon Powers' figures. John Kaszel, Director of Academic Affairs and Research at the Investment Funds Institute of Canada also believes that many fund companies in Canada have been able to reduce the MERs of their funds since the start of the 1990s. The growth in the asset size of these funds has brought about better economies of scale. However, offsetting this trend to lower MERs, the number of new domestic and international equity funds, due to their smaller size and the use of third-party advice, have caused the MER averages for the industry as a whole to rise.

Mr. Hands also indicated that, at present, many 12b-1 fees in the U.S. are running at a very lofty 1% per year; 0.25% for service fees (the Canadian equivalent of trailer fees) and 0.75% for distribution fees. Because these fees are not bundled into the MER numbers for U.S. mutual funds, it creates a very misleading comparison with Canadian mutual fund MERs. Comments made on this subject by Earl Bederman of Investor Economics Inc. reveal just how difficult the comparison of fees between Canadian and U.S. mutual funds can be. Bederman claims that in the U.S. many more no-load funds are purchased by investors through brokerage houses as part of a managed money program. While the MERs are lower on these kinds of funds, the financial advisor will often charge the client an annual fee ranging from 1% to 1.5% of the total assets, which puts fees more in line with those paid by Canadian fundholders.

Finally, it is important to know that if you want to transfer from one fund to another within a fund family, the broker or the dealer usually does have the discretion to charge as much as 2% for doing so. This charge is negotiable and can be lowered to 0% in many cases. The fund may also charge a small percentage fee for moving from one fund to another if it is done within seven days of the first purchase. The purpose of the latter fee is to discourage investors who try to time the market and, in the process, increase the fund's processing costs.

Key Points

- Sales fees are **negotiable**.

- Always check the fund's **Management Expense Ratio** (MER). Funds with **lower MERs** may tend to do **better**.

- Before buying a fund, find out all the **fees** that are charged on **purchase**, **redemption**, **transfer** and **holding** of the fund.

Notes:

[1] John C. Bogle, *Bogle on Mutual Funds*, p. 198. New York: Dell Publishing.
[2] John C. Bogle, *Bogle on Mutual Funds*, p. 198. New York: Dell Publishing.

Chapter 8

How Taxes and Inflation Affect Your Mutual Fund Returns

There are two ways in which mutual funds are taxed. The first is through a direct tax on all forms of gains made by a mutual fund holder (specifically, interest, dividends and capital gains). The other, more indirect, way is through inflation. A short discussion of inflation is in order.

Inflation

Inflation is often called an invisible tax because it is a form of wealth destruction that erodes an individual's purchasing power. The reason that inflation exists, in conventional terms, is because there is an imbalance between supply and demand (too much money buying too few goods). When demand for a product or products is greater than supply, prices will rise. But this explanation does little to explain the sharp rise in inflation over the past thirty years in most of the world's developed nations. Much of this inflation can be attributed to the fact that very few nations have been able to run balanced budgets, i.e. most governments have spent more money than they have taken in, and have covered part of the difference by printing money.

In effect, many nations have been living with an artificially high standard of living that will eventually have to be paid for either through higher taxes and less spending by government, or by increasing the money supply and paying back the debt in devalued currency (or by a combination of these two methods). The investor must constantly keep in mind that his or her investment returns have to keep ahead of both inflation and the direct taxes that must be paid when realizing investment gains. Investors in Canada might be shocked to know that the Bank of Canada created, for the yearly period up to July 1997, new money vastly exceeding what a growing economy needs. In other words, they increased the money supply 5.2%, thus diluting the value of existing dollars. Milton Friedman, one of the great economists of our time, believes that the money supply should grow roughly in proportion to the total output of real Gross Domestic Product (GDP), which was 1.5% this past year and 2.88% over the past 25 years in Canada. Over the past year, M1 has grown 18%, which is a very good leading indicator of inflation. A non-inflationary growth rate in M1 should be currently in the 1.5% to 3% range.

How Governments Tax Inflation

In 1984, the Progressive Conservative government in Canada brought in a one-time $500,000 capital gains exemption for each individual. This meant that an individual in Canada was allowed to make $500,000 in capital gains from investments before any tax would have to be paid on those capital gains. In 1988, the exempt amount was scaled back to $100,000, and by 1994 the capital gains exemption had been completely eliminated by the Liberals. Currently, 75% of capital gains made on investments by Canadians are taxable at the investor's marginal tax rate and any capital losses can only be offset against capital gains. As we shall see below, what this situation effectively does is tax inflation. If we assume that inflation will continue in the years ahead, the additional rate of return necessary to keep ahead of it is significant.

For example, up until 1994 an investor in a 50% tax bracket could earn up to $100,000 tax-free in the form of capital gains. At that time, an investment of $10,000 achieving a 7% capital gain for the year, with inflation for the year being 3%, would end up with a net real return of $400 or 4%. Given the same scenario for 1997, the same investor, after a 75% taxation of the gain at a 50% marginal tax rate and 3% inflation, would currently be left with $437.50 before inflation and $137.50 after inflation (or a rate of return of 1.38%). Because the government doesn't take inflation into account in its taxing policies, the investor is effectively paying tax on a 3% portion of his or her gain when in reality this 3% isn't a gain at all because of inflation. The differential in this situation is significant, and when it is compounded over the next 20 to 30 years it represents a tremendous loss to the investor in return potential.

1997 Tax Rates for Top Tax Bracket Canadians			
	Interest Income %	Dividend Income %	Capital Gains %
British Columbia	54.17	36.58	40.63
Alberta	46.07	31.40	34.55
Saskatchewan	51.95	36.51	38.96
Manitoba	50.40	36.33	37.80
Ontario	51.64	34.87	38.73
Quebec	53.01	38.79	39.76
New Brunswick	51.05	34.48	38.29
Nova Scotia	49.98	33.75	37.49
Prince Edward Island	50.30	33.97	37.73
Newfoundland	53.33	36.01	40.00
Yukon Territory	46.55	31.43	34.91
Northwest Territories	44.37	29.96	33.28

The figures in the above table include the 3% (plus 5% for higher incomes) federal surtax, and provincial surtaxes and flat taxes.

Compounded at a real rate of 4%, the $10,000 would be worth $21,911.23 in 20 years as compared with $13,153.60 under the 1.38% scenario.

How can you protect your after-tax rate of return? One way is through the maximum use of your RRSP, which allows a tax deferral and tax-free compounding on investments until the money is withdrawn. Another way is through maximizing your capital gains and dividend income, as they are taxed at a lower rate than interest income. For mutual fund buyers, capital gains, dividend income and interest income are all paid out to the mutual fund holder and are taxed in the fundholder's hands. More specifically, when capital gains are realized by a fund (when the fund sells a stock in its portfolio at a profit), the fundholder is paid out his or her share of these gains at year end (some funds may have a different year end period). Stocks in a fund that are above their purchase price at year end and are still held by the fund, are termed "unrealized capital gains," and no tax is payable until the stocks are sold.

This is a very important distinction, and has particular relevance when mutual funds are purchased outside of RRSPs. In contrast to capital gains, all interest and dividend income is realized upon receipt by the fund and is usually paid out at year end.

It is important to note that the term "mutual fund dividend" implies a payment to the unitholder that includes capital gains realized by stock sales within the fund, dividend income paid by the stocks held within the fund, and any interest income earned by cash or bonds within the fund.

Important Rules for Purchasing Mutual Funds

Because of the way mutual funds are taxed, it is imperative that the fund buyer know how and when to buy mutual funds so as to maximize the gains received and minimize the tax paid. Poor timing of a purchase, or neglecting to determine the net capital gains and unrealized capital gains within a fund can cost the investor dearly. It can be reasonably assumed that most investors do not understand how the taxes on mutual funds are determined, because there is very little information available on the subject. The following summary addresses the major points regarding proper mutual fund purchasing (for funds outside of an RRSP), with recommendations as to how to maximize return and minimize taxation.

Buy the Mutual Fund Early in the Calendar Year

If one purchases and then sells the same mutual fund during the taxation year (i.e. January 1 through December 31), the price gain or loss will be deemed to be a capital gain or loss. This statement assumes that no dividend was paid out during the year (i.e. there was no capital gain, dividend or interest declared before December 31). This buy and sell situation was often advantageous for the fund buyer who had the use of the $100,000 lifetime capital gains exemption before the 1994 federal budget, because all of this gain (if the gain was under $100,000 and not all of the exemption was previously declared) would be tax-free.

The strategy of buying early in the year and selling at year end before any dividend is paid also allows the investor to claim the entire gain as a capital gain, even though a large part of the fund's appreciation may be due to interest income gains. This allows preferential tax treatment as 75% of the gain is taxable at the investor's marginal tax rate as opposed to the 100% taxability of the interest if the investor waits to receive the year-end dividend payment that will show the amount of interest earned by the fund. It is important to note that many mutual funds that have a large fixed income component may pay a quarterly dividend (and thus present the tax break-down for the investor quarterly) but some still only pay annually. This situation is significant for investors as it can allow for a safer investment in mutual funds with a large fixed income component that can be taxed as a capital gain.

Never Buy a Mutual Fund Late in the Year or Immediately Before a Dividend Payment

When investors buy a mutual fund, their adjusted cost base is the dollar price that they pay for a unit. For example, if the investor buys a fund at a cost of $10 per unit on December 31, that price will be recorded as the initial purchase price. However, the very next day, the fund will pay out the year end dividend (the capital gains realized by the fund over the past year, and the dividends and interest received). Given this example, if the fund had realized $2 per unit in capital gains over the year (on investments sold within the fund for a profit) then this purchaser would be responsible for paying tax on this $2 gain (despite the fact that the investor never really received that gain!) In theory, the investor now has less of his or her capital invested, because Revenue Canada takes taxes on the $2 gain, which of course effectively reduces the amount of capital working for this individual. So this investor would have to pay the tax on $2 of the fund purchase and still have a $10 initial purchase price even though the value of the fund would be $8 starting on January 1 of the following year. Because the fund must pay out the gains earned by the fund each year, the fund will start the next year at a net asset value reflecting the drop in value corresponding to the amount that has been paid out (in the example above, $2 in gains were paid out on December 31). Many investors choose to have this pay-out reinvested automatically, so that they are issued new shares in the fund at a cost (in this example) of $8. The same scenario would also apply to gains on interest and dividend income within the fund.

Check the Amount of Unrealized Capital Gains in the Fund before Purchasing

When an investor buys into a fund, he or she pays the net asset value price per share on that day. For example, if the fund is valued at $10 per share, then the investor pays $10. The make-up of the holdings in the fund, however, is very important because a part of the holdings in the fund may have a future potential tax liability. In the example just given, it is possible that some of the stocks held in the fund will have gone up considerably in value. However, there is no tax to be paid until they are sold. So the adjusted cost price of the fund may be $7, but there will be $3 of tax liability for which the fund purchaser will ultimately be responsible.

Conversely, it is possible for a fund to have unrealized capital losses, so that an investor could potentially purchase a fund at $10, while the adjusted cost base of that fund might actually be $13. In this case, the next $3 of gains would not be taxed, as those gains would only take the fund back to its original cost price. The numbers necessary to calculate the fund's realized and unrealized gains are available from the fund company and should be examined carefully.

A Toronto-based money manager recently announced that an attempt will be made, for his fund, to link the fund purchasers' adjusted cost base more closely to the capital gains (or losses) with which those purchasers are credited. While not providing any details about how they will do this (they have a proprietary arrangement in place and need not disclose) the fund managers admit that the current taxation method can often be unfair to buyers, so they are implementing this program to better serve their clients.

Multiple Purchases and Dollar-Cost Averaging Can't Help

The mutual fund investor should always keep the potential benefits of multiple purchases and dollar-cost averaging in mind. Many mutual fund buyers often reinvest the dividends that they receive into additional shares. In doing so they create a new adjusted cost base for the average price of all their shares. Unfortunately, for tax purposes the investor who redeems or sells part of his or her shares must use the adjusted cost price and cannot control which specific purchases he sells. E.g. if the investor bought the fund at $2, $10 and $11, (100 shares at each purchase) and then sells 100 shares at $12, the adjusted cost base of the shares (in this case $7.76) must be used, as opposed to the investor choosing to sell the shares that were most recently purchased at $11. The difference in capital gain realized in this instance is $4.34, versus $1 if the investor could choose which purchase he or she decided to sell. Many may view this situation as unfair.

Consider the Rate of Turnover of the Fund

The rate at which the portfolio investments turn over within the mutual fund can have a significant impact on the tax consequences for the fund investor. The more a fund manager trades in and out of stocks (or bonds for that matter), the greater the realized taxable gains consequences will be. **The average rate of portfolio turnover for U.S. equities is an incredible 91%. (i.e. 91% of the assets in a fund are changed over the course of a year, with tremendous tax consequences).**[1] Ideally, investors who wish to minimize the tax consequences of their fund purchase should seek out funds with a low portfolio turnover. (Having said that, there is no correlation between overall pre-tax return and portfolio turnover rate.) John Bogle presents a very interesting example of these tax consequences on mutual fund performance over a 10-year period.[2]

From 1967 to 1977, when the average returns for stock mutual funds were negative, most funds realized 100% of the capital gains within the portfolio. That is, while the fund's net asset values were actually lower in 1977, any stocks that went up in the funds over the ten-year period were sold and thus taxes were payable on these gains. (Obviously there were more stocks that went down over this period, but the losses on these stocks were not realized with enough frequency to offset the realized capital gains.) Bogle claims that the average $10,000 fund investment in 1967 would only have been worth $9,120 by 1977, but that there was $2,330 in capital gains realized (with tax being payable on this amount), even though the fund lost money over that ten-year period! Also notable at this time was the high inflation rate that helped erode a large part of the U.S. dollar's purchasing power.[3]

Recently, TD Quantitative Capital (a division of the Toronto Dominion bank) did a study that showed how dramatically a high portfolio turnover affects an investor's after-tax rate of return. When an index fund with a low portfolio turnover rate was compared to a fund with a much higher turnover, it was found that the index fund had a 2.7% higher annual rate of return over a 20-year period.[4]

Things to Think About

Finally, it must be noted that mutual fund managers manage with the sole intent of getting the best rate of return for the fund. They do not pay much attention to the tax consequences of their management style, since every individual investor within the fund has a different personal tax situation. Furthermore, the only statistic that is required to be shown is their overall performance record, which is usually the single most effective factor in attracting investors to a fund. So it remains the responsibility of investors to understand the potential tax consequences to which they will be subject under any given fund manager. A fund investor has much less control than the investor who is simply holding common shares. The investor holding common shares has complete control over his or her capital gain situation. The example, cited above, of funds losing money between 1967 and 1977, but nevertheless incurring taxes on capital gains, is a dramatic illustration of the possible effects of not having control over one's capital gains. Taxes, as it is often stated, have the power to destroy!

Taxes can have a considerable effect on the decision of when to sell a holding. Investors may hold an investment, even though they believe they should sell, because they do not want to realize the gains they have made. Yet if they hold this stock or fund and it drops, they give back (in paper terms) some of the gains they could have realized. This makes investing all the more difficult because, in reality, it distorts the whole free market system by forcing individuals to make investment decisions based not only on pure valuation, but also on the specific tax consequences that result from the sale.

Key Points

- **Inflation** and **taxes** can take a large bite out of investment returns.

- There are several ways to **minimize taxes** through **strategic buying and selling** of mutual funds.

- **Buy funds early in the year** (you can sell them later in the year and the gain will be taxable entirely as a capital gain)

- **Never buy funds late in the year** (you may incur large tax liabilities even though the gain that the tax is payable on was included in the price of your units).

- **Avoid funds with large unrealized capital gains.** (Newly-created funds don't have any unrealized capital gains.)

- Look for funds with **unrealized capital losses.**

- Be **wary** of funds with **high turnover rates** (they usually have **greater realized capital gains**, and you will end up paying more **tax**).

Notes:

[1] Jonathan Clements, *Wall Street Journal*, October 6, 1997 p. C16.

[2] John C. Bogle, *Bogle on Mutual Funds.* New York: Dell Publishing.

[3] John C. Bogle, *Financial Post.*

[4] Susan Heinrich, *Financial Post*, May 7.

Chapter 9

Evaluating Equity Mutual Fund Performance

One of the most difficult decisions facing the mutual fund investor is how to analyse and evaluate equity mutual fund performance. The statistics which one might think would give a clear and fair comparison between two similar mutual funds can be misleading and frequently don't represent the whole performance story. A number of different comparisons and measurements are needed to thoroughly evaluate a mutual fund's performance. And even after thorough evaluation, there are no guarantees as to the fund's future performance (as all the disclaimers in prospectuses and advertisements say). Nevertheless it is realistic, I believe, to expect fund managers and fund families with long-term track records showing consistent and superior performance to be able to continue their winning ways in the future.

The total return on an equity mutual fund is the percentage change in the fund's net asset value over a specific period of time, with the final net asset value taking into account reinvestment of all income, dividends and any capital gains distributions made by the fund.[1] It is important to note that these figures do not take into account any of the initial sales charges or the taxes that are paid by the investor. The net asset value of many mutual funds is reported daily in a number of newspapers, and performance calculations are often reported monthly in percentage terms.

An equity mutual fund's performance can be measured and compared in many different ways. Below are some of the most commonly used yardsticks.

Performance vs. the Index

One way to evaluate an equity mutual fund's performance is to compare it to a comparable market index. The major market indexes for equities are often used as a barometer for how well or poorly stocks in general have done. The S&P 500 and the Dow Jones Industrial Average in the U.S., and the TSE 300 in Canada are the most quoted indexes for market performance and many different equity funds' performances are measured against them. While these indexes are upwardly biased by their very nature (see Chapter 15), they do quite often (specifically the S&P 500) give a reasonably realistic evaluation of how equities in general have performed over the shorter term.

As might be expected, the majority of equity mutual funds underperform the major indexes over the longer term (although this does depend on what sources are used and quoted). The most apparent reason for this is the costs of the equity funds. Most equity funds have average annual fees in the 2% range, which means that the fund manager must consistently beat the market index by 2% just to stay even. While it is possible to outperform the indexes over given periods of time, it is very difficult to do so over the longer term. There are, however, fund managers who have been able to do this, and their loyal shareholders have been rewarded handsomely.

One of the difficulties for today's fund buyer is that many of the available mutual funds only came into being in the last five years. In other words, a reliable long-term track record is frequently simply not available. Fund managers may also move around from company to company, so that a fundholder might buy a fund on the basis of its historical performance numbers and end up having the fund managed by someone other than the person who achieved those results. In a recent article in the *Globe and Mail*, Duff Young presented some revealing statistics which further complicate the issue of choosing a fund.[2] He concludes that when star fund managers leave one fund to manage another, their performance at the new fund often does not match their previous success.

The creation of index mutual funds evolved from the generally accepted belief that most funds underperform the index. For many investors, index funds are a viable way to achieve performance comparable to the major indexes. Chapter 15 contains a discussion of the benefits and drawbacks of index funds.

Fund by Fund Comparison

It is common practice to compare different equity mutual funds on the basis of their performance results. How one goes about this, however, is of critical importance. Looking at just the performance numbers can be more than a little deceptive if you don't understand how the numbers were achieved.

Comparing Apples with Apples

One important rule when looking at equity mutual fund performance is to understand the need to compare funds within the same asset class. Given the nature of financial markets, certain funds will outperform other funds based on their specific area or asset class. For example, funds invested in U.S. equities in 1996 have probably done better than most international mutual funds because of the strong U.S. stock markets and a strengthening U.S. dollar. Next year the reverse may be true. It is therefore only realistic and prudent to compare funds within similar asset classes. Without such a comparison, the investor is likely to chase the best performing funds over the short term, which almost always results in poor long-term investment returns.

Even when funds are categorized within the same class (e.g. Canadian or U.S. equity funds), their investment styles may be totally different. For example, one particular money manager of an American equity fund may attempt to rotate in and out of sectors to achieve higher rates of appreciation whereas another may take a value approach, buying undervalued equities and holding them until their full value is realized. The investment objectives of these funds, as set out in their prospectuses, may often appear to be very similar (e.g. long term appreciation etc.) despite the fact that the respective fund managers will approach investing quite differently. It is quite possible for the fund buyer to have no idea of how the different investment approaches will affect the shorter-term volatility of the fund. As a result of these different management styles, the track record measurements can be a little deceptive.

Beta

This term is often used when evaluating or measuring risk when applied to investment portfolios. Beta indicates the past price volatility of a fund in relation to a particular stock market index. The general market receives a Beta value of 1; funds that are more volatile than the general market will have Betas higher than 1, and less volatile funds will have Betas of less than 1. Most general equity funds will have Betas in the range of 0.85 to 1.05.[3] For example, a fund with a Beta of 0.80 might be expected to fall 8% when the general market drops 10% and rise 8% when the market rises 10%. Conversely, a fund with a 1.20 Beta can be expected to drop 12% when the market drops 10% and rise 12% on a 10% market increase. The Beta numbers are often included in track record performance and should be examined.

A high Beta mutual fund can often attract a multitude of new buyers after a very successful year. Quite often, following a strong performance year, there is a large increase in the fund's assets as a result of new buyers pouring money into the fund to try to participate in the fund manager's success. Because of the very strong recent one-year performance, the 3-, 5- and sometimes even 10-year performance numbers may also look better. It is quite likely, however, that the fund's high Beta number will show itself in the other direction, and all of the new money that piled in at the highs will be punished when the performance of the fund reverses itself. The often-heard phrase "How come I never seem to get the rates of returns that they show in the paper or advertise on T.V.?" can be a direct result of investing in funds with high Beta numbers and not appreciating the volatility that comes with them. Regression to the mean is a strong tendency that will help explain, to a certain extent, why markets behave the way they do.

Regression to the Mean

This term refers to the strong tendency of total returns of financial assets to regress to the mean (or average performance). This applies to common stocks, asset sectors and equity mutual fund performance, and implies that the shorter-term rates of returns on these assets will eventually move back toward their long-term performance numbers.

In the above-mentioned example of the performance of a high Beta fund, the shorter-term performance numbers of the fund would have shown results well above the equity fund long-term performance mean. Unfortunately, the investors that bought the fund after its great one-year performance would not have received very good returns. All too often this pattern of chasing hot funds and managers is repeated, with similar results. (In the fund buyer's defence, it is fair to say that in some instances the mutual fund industry does play a large part in affecting an individual's behaviour by fostering certain beliefs with regard to fund performance through the large amount of advertising done while performance is still strong.)

Warren Buffett, one of America's great investors, often warns shareholders of the company he controls, Berkshire Hathaway, not to expect to receive the performance numbers that have been achieved in the past. (Berkshire Hathaway is a holding company which owns large positions in a number of American companies, making it much like a closed end mutual fund.) If Berkshire Hathaway was to maintain its historic rate of growth, Buffett warns, it would not be long before it owned everything on the planet! While this is obviously an impossibility, Buffet's attitude nicely illustrates the well-founded belief that regression to the mean (or in the Berkshire Hathaway example, a *little* closer to the mean) eventually must happen. The difficulty usually lies in predicting just *when* that will start to happen.

Interestingly, this was echoed by Sir John Templeton at the 1997 Templeton Funds annual meeting, who stated that "patient investors should expect to receive 10% rates of return for the next 43 years, compared with 15.5% in the past 43 years for holders of the Templeton Growth Fund."

Understanding the principle of regression to the mean is of paramount importance to investors in financial markets and mutual funds. When equity markets are hitting new highs, and when the market confidence that goes hand-in-hand with that success is peaking, it is imperative that investors proceed very cautiously.

When Will This Market Regress Back To the Mean?

It is important to remember that markets can move from periods of extreme euphoria to terrible bouts of depression. When things are positive, it is often very difficult to visualize or remember that things were once not *quite* as good. In addition, the longer the good markets (or the bad ones) continue, the more the perception is reinforced that the *status quo* will go on for a long time, or possibly even forever! A phrase that is often heard is: "This time it's different". It may indeed be different this time, but the odds are that it's not.

The present market situation in North America is extremely positive. Equities are performing well and money continues to flow into equity funds at unprecedented levels. Many investment advisors are even recommending that investors remortgage their homes and put this money into mutual funds. Their argument is based on the fact that real estate is doing poorly and that equity prices continue to rise. Are they correct? And are investors who are not currently invested in equity markets missing the boat? Perhaps. However, an examination of some of the current data relating to market valuation reveals some very interesting points. For example, the long-term rate of return on equities is generally around 11%. The equity markets from 1993 to 1996 have achieved a growth rate of approximately 17%. (As of mid-1997, it is higher still.) It is quite likely that this rate of growth is unsustainable.

Another interesting fact is that the price/dividend ratio on the S&P 500 has recently hit a record high of 62.11. This statistic represents a hard number, in that investors are paying $62.11 for $1.00 of dividends, which in effect gives a yield of 1.61%. The previous high was seen in 1987 when the ratio was 38, and most readers know what happened in October of that year. Richard Russell notes that up until the 1970s, any time the price/dividend ratio rose as high as 34 to 36, it signalled a top for over-valuation of stocks, and a bear market or large market price drop quickly followed.[4]

Finally, the price to earnings ratios (the price one pays for current earnings) on all major stock indexes in the mid 1990s have flirted with, or are achieving, all-time highs. It appears that the shareholders of the companies that trade on these exchanges are paying substantial premiums for the prospect of continued growth. This expected growth must be delivered or prices will eventually adjust to the reality.

Although these historical yardsticks show market over-valuation, there are probably just as many other new or modern valuation models used by money managers that can show how this particular market, or equities within this market, are undervalued. That's what makes investing so interesting: for every buyer who believes a stock is going to go up, there is usually a seller who believes it is going to go down.

R-Squared

This term is used to explain or define a mutual fund's return or performance in relation to the underlying market that it has been invested in (i.e. Japanese equity mutual funds compared to the Nikkei Index, or U.S. growth funds compared to the S&P 500 Index). Specifically, the market index that the mutual fund is measured against is given a value of 1. Most basic mutual funds have an R-Squared around 80% to 90%, meaning that 80% to 90% of a fund's performance is related to the underlying market in which it is invested. In other words about 10% to 20% of a fund's performance numbers result from the management skills and strategies applied to buying and selling within the fund's portfolio.

It is important to understand this, because it is not uncommon for investors to look at a fund's track record and (perhaps falsely) draw the conclusion that the fund's great performance was the direct result of excellent management. This situation is not uncommon for sector funds that can have spectacular results simply because of a boom in the primary markets in which they invest. Most recently, the Far East (in the minds of many investors) became a great market to invest in because of its move toward capitalism and its largely untapped labour resources. Initially, investors who bought mutual funds in this sector did extremely well. In fact, because of the strong stock market performance of companies listed on the Far East exchanges, almost all of the funds invested in these markets did extremely well. The mutual fund industry, seeing the public's appetite for Far East mutual funds, began a large push into this area by starting many more of these funds.

After the initial excitement and the great performance of these stocks listed in the Far East, mutual funds in this sector have largely underperformed. The reason for the downturn is not simply that the managers of these funds have lost their touch, as many investors might assume. The fact is that equity markets in the Far East have in general come down significantly since the highs of the early 1990s. Remembering that fund managers may often be under pressure to stay fully invested at all times, it is not hard to understand why these funds have done poorly recently. A recent *Wall Street Journal* article highlighted this situation, revealing that some fund managers are actually buying put options (a method of selling) on stocks and indexes for their own personal accounts while keeping investors fully invested in the funds that they manage. The pressure from fundholders to stay fully invested is the reason the fund managers are sticking around in today's equity markets.[5] So, investors must decide for themselves whether they wish to be fully invested in such markets, or properly diversified by including this specific sector in their overall portfolio. Fund managers won't get you out, and you should not expect them to.

Emerging Funds Performance Summary: Index v. All Funds			
	1993	**1994**	**1995**
MSCI Emerging Market Index	82.3%	-1.8%	-7.8%
All Emerging Funds	70.3%	-9.7%	-10.8%

The above chart shows how closely the performance of all the funds designated as "emerging market" follows the overall emerging market index (while underperforming it).

In conclusion on the subject of R-squared, the investor can see that a large proportion of a fund's performance can be attributed to the market(s) invested in, as opposed to the fund manager's stock picking ability. That of course raises the question of whether a basket of index funds will not do as well as, or better than, a fund. The answer to that depends on various factors. Many fund managers do manage money essentially by attempting to rotate in and out of sectors depending on their overall market evaluations. In this case, successful managers can add real value for shareholders. It may be possible for individuals to meet with success by doing this themselves, although it is probably better to balance many different types of funds in differing markets and asset classes, and to hold them over the longer, rather than shorter, term. In many instances, index funds can be used to reduce overall management costs, potentially without sacrificing any significant gains. The R-squared statistics bear this out.

Alpha

This term relates the amount of risk taken by the fund manager, in terms of the fund's Beta, and adjusts it to the fund's total return. A positive Alpha reflects good performance whereas a negative Alpha denotes poor performance. In essence, this measurement attempts to show the buyer how good the fund manager is by relating the performance to the risk taken. For example, a conservatively managed or low-risk fund that achieves rates of return superior to those expected on the basis of the fund's Beta, would score well or have a positive Alpha. Conversely, a fund with a high Beta and an aggressive money management style, but with lower rates of return than should be achieved given the risk taken, would have a negative Alpha.

There are money management styles and theories that do incorporate the Alpha measurement philosophy and concept in determining a proper asset mix. For example, using past performance data on many different asset classes (Canadian and U.S. stocks, foreign bonds and equities, domestic bonds, etc.) a model can be designed so as to maximize the expected return to the investor based upon the investor's desired level of risk. The chart below shows the risk/reward relationship, where the goal is to get as close to the curve as possible. (The curve represents the highest theoretical rate of return, given the risk taken.) Over time, the performance of the asset mix is reasonably consistent because of the diversity of the portfolio and the longer-term historical relationship between these asset classes.

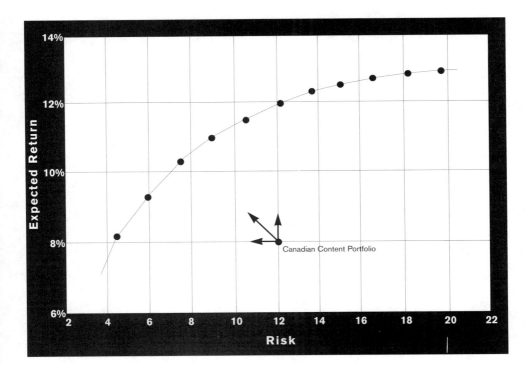

The above chart also illustrates how diversification for a Canadian investor can increase a portfolio's rate of return while at the same time decreasing the amount of risk taken. By simply adding foreign equities and assets, a Canadian investor can increase the rate of return and decrease the risk of the portfolio (as indicated by the long arrow on the above graph). The optimal asset mix for a Canadian investor is generally $1/3$ of total portfolio value in foreign securities (with the remaining two thirds in Canadian assets). Investors should keep this relationship in mind when designing their portfolios.

Mutual Fund Size

It has been argued that when a mutual fund gets to be too large, its performance numbers may suffer because its manager lacks the ability to get in and out of stock positions efficiently. This may be the case if the manager has to sell too much stock for the market to absorb, or if he or she is unable to buy a sufficient amount of stock at the right price. Although this is a logical argument, it is not borne out by a comparison of the performance numbers of large and small mutual funds. It should be noted, however, that a fund that is too small runs the risk of having much higher expense ratios because of a lack of economies of scale (i.e. all the expenses of running the fund are supported by a much smaller asset base). Fund buyers should therefore be careful when considering very small or newly launched funds.

Key Points

- There are many ways to **compare the performance** of different mutual funds. Where possible, use them all!

- Make sure you **compare funds** that hold **similar assets** and that have **similar objectives**.

- Make sure you understand how a fund's **Alpha** and **Beta** numbers can be used to better evaluate the fund's performance.

- The **R-Squared** number illustrates how closely a **fund's performance** is correlated to the **underlying market** in which it is invested.

- Canadian investors can increase their rate of return and decrease the amount of risk by investing in **foreign assets**.

- **Regression to the mean** is the tendency for all investments to return to their **historical rates of return**.

- There is **no correlation** between the **size** of a fund (its asset value in dollars) and its **performance**.

Notes:

[1] John Bogle, *Bogle on Mutual Funds*, p. 61.

[2] Duff Young, *The Globe & Mail.*

[3] John C. Bogle, *Bogle on Mutual Funds*, p. 82. New York: Dell Publishing.

[4] Richard Russell, *Dow Theory Letters*, October 23, 1996.

[5] *Wall Street Journal*, Monday, December 30, 1996.

Chapter 10

Long-Term Track Records for Equity Mutual Funds

A statement that is often heard is that stocks or equity investments tend to outperform bonds and cash over the long term. The performance of the stock indexes (their shortfalls being noted) show a clearly superior rate of return when compared with the long-term performance of bonds and cash. But the question that is probably most important to individual investors is how mutual funds themselves have done over the long term.

In This Chapter:

- **Why is it Hard to Find Many Equity Mutual Funds with Long-Term Track Records?**

- **Merging and Consolidation of Funds**

- **Mutual Fund Buyouts**

- **The Name Game**

- **Conclusion**

Why is it Hard to Find Many Equity Mutual Funds with Long-Term Track Records?

What few people realize is that many mutual funds have come and gone over the last 70 years, so it is nearly impossible to know how an individual who had put his or her money into funds back in the early years would have fared. It's my opinion that most investors probably wouldn't have done very well. There are several reasons that may lead others to the same conclusion.

Merging and Consolidation of Funds

When two or more mutual funds combine or merge, the track record of the better fund is used for historical performance reporting. This situation gives rise to a term known as "survivorship bias," which means that only funds still alive in their original form are evaluated.

The merging of different funds can be the result of several possible situations. It is not uncommon, when a fund company has many different funds, for it to consolidate some of the smaller funds with the larger funds with similar objectives within the fund family. This will improve the overall expense ratio of the smaller funds. The smaller a fund is, the greater the fixed costs are, on a percentage basis, to the fund. So, in many instances, this consolidation makes sense. But when we look a little deeper, we sometimes see that the funds may be smaller in asset size because they have underperformed other funds in their sector, with a resulting decrease in the influx of new money. It is very unlikely that the fund company would put much advertising muscle behind marketing these poorer performance numbers, so for the most part these funds become orphans. So, once the merger takes place the holders of the original smaller fund will see much better performance numbers on their fund, although they won't really benefit from those numbers!

Mutual Fund Buyouts

Similarly, mutual fund companies will sometimes buy out other fund companies. It is very rare for a fund company to go bankrupt (and even if it did, the fundholders' assets are segregated), but some fund companies do of course underperform relative to other fund companies. Over time a poorer performer will experience more withdrawals than purchases as fund investors look for better performers. It is quite likely that these withdrawals will contribute to the fund's underperformance, since the fund manager is forced to sell stocks in the portfolio (possibly at a bad time) to raise cash for the redemptions.

At this point, it is often advantageous for the fund company to look for potential buyers. The assets that the underperforming fund has under administration represent future revenue dollars to somebody, and if a different company comes in and buys control of these assets it may be possible to keep most of the existing fundholders' money. A buyout in this situation is almost always portrayed as a positive development. It also gives new hope to the fundholders of funds managed by the previous company. At this point the underperforming mutual funds will often be merged with the funds of the acquiring company and, in the process, the poor track records will disappear.

The Name Game

Another technique used to salvage underperforming mutual funds is simply to shut them down and transfer them to a new name. The manager of the fund, or the fund company itself, doesn't change; the only change is in the name of the fund or family of funds. With this kind of name change, the past performance records usually disappear.

While not specifically related to long-term performance, the dividends paid at the end of each year by funds (the realized capital gains, dividends and interest earned by those funds) are often issued as additional shares. The fundholder who receives these shares starts the new year with additional shares and the market value of these shares drops to reflect the dividends that have been paid out. Over time, it can be easy to forget or become confused about how much money was initially invested and how this investment is actually performing. This problem can also be compounded when the investor is buying shares on a monthly or quarterly basis. It is entirely likely that, because of this process of paying dividends in the form of shares, many investors will have real difficulty in determining how well their funds are really performing.

Conclusion

The importance of noting these scenarios is to highlight how difficult it is to determine long-term money manager performance. There are many good mutual fund companies and just as many good fund managers, and their track records speak for themselves, but the investing public rarely sees the past records (or any evidence) of the poorer funds. All it takes to drive an investor's overall portfolio rate of return down to levels similar to bonds or cash yields (or below them for that matter) is to have one bad fund. And because of the cyclical nature of mutual fund performance and popularity, it is more than likely that many investors will end up with at least one very bad fund during the course of those cycles.

In examining all of the long-term data available on equity and equity mutual fund performance, it is still unclear what one can and should expect from investing in this area. The president of a large fund company in the U.S. commented recently on "*Wall Street Week*" that equity mutual funds' return over inflation has probably been about 3% over the long term. Although this is a very subjective number, it is probably quite realistic. For individuals who feel that this figure may be on the low side, investing in equity funds (as opposed to cash or bonds) is an easy decision because of equity funds' greater potential for gain. For skeptics, who have had bad experiences in the markets and equity funds, this number may seem very high or even unrealistic. In the latter case, index funds, bonds or cash may be arguably a better home for their investments. With both the U.S. and Canada offering real return bonds with yields at around 3% and 4.25% above inflation respectively, there are investment products currently available that have yields similar to long-term equity mutual fund peformance numbers, yet with much lower risk levels.

Key Points

- Finding **equity mutual funds** with **long track records** can be difficult because of the **number of funds that have come and gone** over the last 70 years.

- When two or more **funds merge,** the **track record of the better fund** is used for historical performance reporting.

- Smaller funds may be **merged into bigger funds** within the same company, sometimes giving the **appearance** (but not the reality) of **better performance figures**.

- An **underperforming fund or fund company** may be **acquired by another company**, effectively **erasing the fund's poor track record.**

- **Poor performance records** may sometimes be **effectively hidden** by shutting down a family of funds and **transferring it to a new name** (without changing the fund manager or company.)

- **Dividends** paid at the end of each year by funds are often **issued and received as additional shares**, sometimes making it **difficult to calculate** exactly **how well a particular fund is doing** for an investor choosing this form of payment.

Chapter 11

Comparing Equity Mutual Funds to Other Asset Classes

It is common to compare the performance of equities or equity mutual funds to the performance of other asset classes. An individual who has an amount of money to invest often has a difficult decision in trying to choose the best place to put it. Should you buy more real estate or pay down the existing mortgage? Should you buy gold or put the money into bonds? Should you buy equity mutual funds?

There is no one correct answer to these questions despite what anyone may say. All of these asset classes have the ability to outperform or underperform each other over a given period of time. Interestingly enough, it is only mutual funds that do not have a measurable long-term performance record, as we have seen previously.

Blanket statements about certain types of investments and their respective merits are often made to investors. Some of the most common of these blanket statements are: "GICs or bonds are no good," "equity mutual funds outperform bonds or cash," and "why rent when you can pay yourself by buying a house". Investors can be confused by all the different opinions they hear or the financial information they read. When a particular asset class is doing well in relation to other classes, the general consensus is that the better-performing asset class is without doubt the best place to be at that time. At the present time this appears to be true of equity mutual funds.

Proponents of the contrarian investment philosophy would say that it is precisely when the masses are buying funds by the truckload, that they are the worst place to be. Only time will tell!

Below is a brief description of several asset class alternatives to equities and equity mutual funds.

Real Estate

If we look at the long-term track record of real estate prices, it becomes obvious that it is an unpredictable and cyclical asset. There have been times in history when, over a 100-year period, the price of real estate has largely remained unchanged (e.g. in several European countries in recent centuries). There have also been times when real estate has achieved tremendous rates of return over periods stretching as far as 30 to 40 years. In more recent times, (specifically, since the Second World War) real estate prices have, in general in North America outperformed most asset classes, with prices finally peaking in the late 1980s.

Much of this growth may be attributed to the population growth in Canada and the U.S. over this time, with favourable demographic numbers helping to fuel real estate demand for houses and all forms of commercial property. It has not been a straight line up over this time, however, as economic downturns have been particularly hard on certain areas (such as Texas real estate prices in the early 1980s) over this period. Many U.S. cities have experienced downward price pressures as crime and urban housing projects have resulted in major migrations of people to surrounding suburbs and counties.

Since the peak of real estate prices at the start of the 1990s, real estate has underperformed most asset classes and has significantly underperformed inflation in most cases. There are certain areas that have experienced price appreciation (such as Vancouver) but they are the exception rather than the rule.

Because of real estate's recent poor performance, people are no longer bombarded with the advertisements or infomercials that were common in the 1980s. People such as Tom Vu or Ed Beckley promised great riches in real estate through their proven systems (buy distressed properties and use lots of leverage) and it is quite likely that anybody who did follow their advice has long since declared bankruptcy. Ironically, there are many advisors now telling people to remortgage their homes and buy equity mutual funds, the logic being that real estate will not go up and equity mutual funds will. In these instances the use of leverage poses very real risks. "But the people who make these recommendations sound so confident and convincing," one can almost hear the investor say, "How can they be wrong?" Well, not only can they be wrong, there's a good chance that they will be wrong. And if they are wrong, remember that it's not their money, its yours! Besides, most people have short memories, and these promoters are quite likely to return with new recommendations every few years. One popular investment advisor in Canada declared personal bankruptcy only a couple of years ago, and yet still packs the rooms where he speaks! He is, by the way, currently advising people to buy equity mutual funds.

Real Estate's Advantages

There are some real tax advantages to owning real estate. The principal residence rule allows tax-free appreciation for most homeowners. This can serve the dual purpose of acting as a forced savings plan for new homeowners, since the money required for interest and principal must be paid monthly (in most cases) which contributes to the equity value in the home. It is worth noting, however, that the mortgage interest payments are not tax deductible. As a result it is most often advisable to pay off the mortgage as quickly as possible. Because of the high tax rate on other investment gains (i.e. capital gains on stocks and equity mutual funds) a very high rate of return on these investments is needed to offset the non tax-deductible interest payments if one decides to minimize mortgage payments and invest the difference.

Another benefit to home ownership is that the home is not an asset that is valued every day. The anxiety of watching volatile price fluctuations on stocks can be stressful for investors and can often lead to bad decisions. The homeowner is spared this stress and as a result can probably sleep better and make rational decisions regarding property sale and purchase. In many instances, a home is also more of a lifestyle investment than a way to make money. A poorly-timed purchase of a house as a lifestyle investment can, however, quickly become an ever-increasing financial stress factor if similar houses in the neighbourhood are sold for much lower prices thereafter.

Canadian Residential Real Estate Performance

Ups and downs in house prices

% Annual percentage change in average house price by city.

	Calgary	Montreal	Toronto	Vancouver

Source: The Canadian Real Estate Association

From "*Real Estate on the Rise*", Rob Carrick, *The Globe and Mail*, Saturday April 19, 1997, p. B22.

Real Estate's Disadvantages

On the flip side of the coin, there are several disadvantages to owning real estate. First, there are property taxes to be paid. Maintenance and other costs of upkeep may also consume considerable amounts of cash. But probably the greatest drawback to real estate ownership is illiquidity. As many purchasers of tax-driven condominium deals found out, there are certain times when there may be no bids at all for properties for sale. At this point the carrying costs can really add up. Even if tenants can be found to rent the premises, there are many potential headaches that come with being a landlord.

In terms of purchasing a home, the down payment often represents most, if not all, of the life savings of the buyer. Outside of possible RRSP contributions, many people have all of their assets in one investment: their house. In a rising real estate market, this can be all right, but if the property only maintains its value or if the value heads down, then the leverage used on the investment (i.e. the mortgage) can, in reality, clobber the owner. In Texas for example, many individuals walked away from their houses many years after the initial purchase with the mortgage value considerably larger than the current market value of the property.

Another question that must be raised is whether the capital gains exemption on a principal residence will remain in force over the coming years. While many people believe that the government could never take it away (there would be a popular uprising!) the same thing had been said about Old Age Security (OAS) benefits. OAS benefits are now available only to Canadians who are 65 or older and who earn less than $53,215 a year while retired. This means that individuals who have (indirectly) contributed to the plan for years won't receive anything if their retirement income is above $53,215. The same may eventually be true for the Canada Pension Plan (CPP). Furthermore, in 1996 the federal government lowered the age for RRSP conversion into RRIF or annuity, from 71 to 69. This was yet another of the federal government's tax grabs in their ever-increasing need for additional revenues. So it is quite possible that the principal residence exemption may be eliminated, in whole or in part, in future years.

Buy or Rent?

One of the principal questions that comes up when discussing real estate is whether to buy or rent. There is no easy answer, but there are some simple considerations. For example, does the purchaser think real estate prices will rise? (For the most part, the answer to that question will be nothing more than an educated guess). Does the person plan on living in the purchased house, or renting it out? One realistic way to evaluate real estate is by the potential yield on the investment. If, for example, a real estate investment, after property taxes and expenses, yields a rate of return that is comparably higher than a safe long-term government bond, then it is quite possible that the price of the real estate is reasonable in terms of alternative investments. Conversely, when buying a property on which the rental yield is considerably lower than current bond yields (outside of luxury properties) then it is quite likely that the asset is fully priced or overvalued. One way out of this problem is to buy a bond and save the headaches. While this is by no means the only way to value real estate, it can put pricing in its proper perspective.

Real Estate Mutual Funds

It is possible to own real estate through mutual funds. There are currently several open-end and closed-end funds that can give investors exposure to commercial and income property. The popularity of real estate funds, however, diminished following the peak of real estate prices in the late 1980s. Several of the open-end realty funds were forced to close off redemption as there was a mad rush of investors all trying to get out of these funds at the same time. Because of the illiquidity of many of the properties held within the funds, there was not enough money to pay all the redemption requests. Some of these funds have changed from open-end to closed-end status, thus giving investors liquidity through the stock market, while allowing the fund managers to keep and manage the investments in the fund without the constant threat of more redemptions. It is worth noting that there are several real estate funds that are still not allowing any redemptions, six years after imposing these restrictions. This is a terrible situation for the investors in those funds as they have no way of accessing their own money.

One positive thing about real estate mutual funds is that you can get exposure to this sector without having to place too much of your personal wealth in the investment. In most instances, there is good liquidity (investors should seriously consider closed-end real estate funds that trade on a major market to avoid possible liquidity problems) and the funds will usually offer good diversification through different kinds of real estate holdings and locations. The rates of return on real estate funds will of course vary depending upon the timing of the purchase and the skill of the manager. In the long term these real estate funds can be quite capable of producing rates of return similar to equity mutual funds.

More recently, Real Estate Investment Trusts have become popular, primarily a result of the fact that they provide an income stream for investors that want higher returns than those provided by traditional bonds or GICs. Much like a closed-end real estate mutual fund, they trade on a stock exchange and invest in income producing properties. Usually, a large percentage of the income is paid out to the fundholder. Considering the high prices of equities these days, these trusts do offer a reasonable investment alternative. It should also be noted that, historically, there is very little correlation between real estate and equity performance.

In concluding the discussion on real estate, mention should be made of how difficult it can be to predict future trends in this sector. In North America, the changing demographics of the population is likely to affect the supply and demand relationship not only of residential housing prices but also of commercial real estate property prices. In addition, the spending and living patterns of many individuals in Canada and the U.S. will undoubtedly change with the aging of the "baby boomer" generation. Finally, the changes occurring as a result of the information age could have a tremendous impact on the traditional office structure of many corporations.

The potential for large numbers of employees to be able to work in any location (e.g. at home), could change the need and demand for office space drastically, with large implications for real estate pricing. Accurately predicting or assessing future real estate trends should prove to be a very interesting and difficult challenge.

Gold and Precious Metals

Gold has traditionally been a form of money. Why gold was chosen over other portable assets or commodities is hard to say, but it may have something to do with its scarcity. On a purely economic scale, the use or need for gold is minimal. In fact, outside of jewellery, there is not much need for gold in today's economy. It is, however, still viewed by many as a form of money that is both portable and easy to store. In many third world and developing nations, where political instability and distrust of ruling regimes or governments is high, gold (along with the U.S. dollar) is in great demand. Many of the paper currencies in these countries quickly become worthless through high inflation or constant changes in the ruling authorities, and gold provides one way of protecting accumulated assets through all of these destabilizing events.

It is said that in the time of Christ, one ounce of gold would purchase 300 loaves of bread. With the gold price currently around $320 (September 1997) U.S., and a loaf of bread costing approximately $1 U.S., one can honestly conclude that gold is a good inflationary hedge over the long term (the very, very long term, that is!). Having said that, gold's performance over the last 15 years has probably been the poorest of any asset class, as the chart below shows.

It is worth noting the sharp rise in the price of gold from 1972 (when the U.S. went off the gold standard) to 1980 when prices peaked. This was an inflationary time, particularly in the U.S., and while gold's popularity as a hedge against inflation was clearly recognized, it is evident with hindsight that gold fever took over and a mania developed that would drive the price of gold bullion to incredible levels. Perhaps investors were worried that high inflation was never going to end and that the price of gold at the time was not fully discounting the rapid inflation that might have seemed destined to continue long into the future. However, as soon as the market came to realize that this scenario was not going to unfold, gold plummeted.

While gold had generally been expected, in the past, to rise in times of inflation or of political crisis, in the last 10 years this has clearly not been the case. Why the price of gold has not been able to crack the $400 U.S. level and stay there is a mystery. One explanation is that every time gold does rally, many of the world's central banks sell more of their gold reserves. This can show some tremendous balance sheet gains for these institutions, which effectively have a lot of their gold on the books at $35 U.S. an ounce. There is also the argument that all of the nations that have been selling gold are doing so to prevent their own paper currencies (which are backed by nothing other than the ability to tax residents and print more money) from showing real weakness against gold. The bottom line is that nobody really knows what is going on. It may in fact be possible that gold's importance within the financial world could slowly be diminishing.

Despite all that, it is probably very prudent for all investors to have at least some form of gold in their portfolios. Gold bullion is nice to have for portability, but unfortunately it doesn't pay any interest for someone holding it in a safety deposit box. A more effective means of gold ownership is through gold stocks or gold mutual funds.

Gold and Precious Metals Companies and Funds

Gold or precious metals companies generally have much better upside potential than the commodities themselves. For example, if a gold producer's cost of production is $200 U.S. an ounce, and the spot price of gold is $400 U.S., the company will make a profit on the differential ($200). If gold rises to $500 an ounce, the company's price differential moves from $200 to $300, a percentage increase of 50%. Compared to holding bullion, a 25% gain, the leverage is considerable. This leverage can obviously work in reverse, where the gold producer's profitability can drop considerably if bullion falls. In analysing major gold producing companies, the cost of production is usually put in relation to the cost per ounce of gold. The cheaper the cost of production per ounce, the higher the market will value the company.

In order to reduce the market risks of gold price fluctuations, gold producers will often sell forward a percentage of their future production, in order to lock in present gold prices. This can reduce operating profit volatility for the gold company, and increases stability for future planning. The forward selling of contracts can in itself affect gold prices and is usually an important component in trying to interpret future gold prices.

Investors can buy senior gold producer stocks outright or participate in the gold sector through buying an industry-specific fund. The gold or precious metals mutual fund allows greater diversification among senior producing gold stocks, as well as the ability to participate in buying intermediate and junior gold producers with properties in the early stages of drilling and exploration. Investing in these smaller gold producers and more speculative companies can give a fund manager the chance of hitting the "mother lode." Because the fund is diversified, small amounts of fund money (in percentage terms) can be invested in these speculative stocks without being a huge drag on fund performance if they don't pan out. If they do, however, the added kick of a stock going up 100-fold can make a real difference in overall returns.

Gold and precious metals funds can be, on average, more volatile than traditional equity funds, so care must be taken to decide how much volatility and fluctuation you can withstand when investing in this asset class. It should be noted that if gold prices ever do run up to the highs they achieved in the early 1980s, these funds could do incredibly well. And even if gold prices stay in their current trading range of $320 U.S. to $350 U.S. per ounce, large appreciation is still possible if a company can increase its efficiency or discover new and economically viable reserves. A skilful money manager who can correctly identify companies with outstanding future potential stands to do very well.

Below are the performance numbers of two gold mutual funds over the past ten years. Despite the sideways movement of the gold bullion price, the funds were able to rack up some very impressive numbers at different times.

LONDON AM GOLD FIX (CDN$)
AS OF MARCH 31, 1997

1 month	3 month	1 year	3 year	5 year	10 year
-1.9%	-4.5%	-10.3%	-3.1%	-3.4%	-1.0%

2 CANADIAN PRECIOUS METAL FUNDS
AS OF MARCH 31, 1997

1 month	3 month	1 year	3 year	5 year	10 year
11.24%	6.9%	15.30%	1.91%	20.09%	7.4%
-12.2%	-6.1%	-12.6%	-26.4%	26%	n/a

Bonds and Bond Funds

It is generally recognized and accepted that, over the long term, equities should out-perform bonds. Like many bold statements and generalizations, this is true in certain instances and false in others. The banking and investment industry has helped in creating, in recent years, the perceived need for investors to purchase equity mutual funds to ensure that maximum rates of return on investment are achieved. Equity mutual fund investment is chiefly advertised and portrayed as the investment norm, particularly for successful people. The advertising also stresses the fact that this kind of investment can be adjusted to meet everyone's needs. The real dangers in this popular view of things is that, in many cases, the expected rates of return will not be achieved by the novice equity and mutual fund investor.

In fact, the investor can quite possibly lose huge amounts of capital in the process. The fact that the major banks now focus more than ever on managed money products and actively promote them through their branches can create a false sense of security in the fund buyer's mind. Some people believe that if the banks are promoting these investments, they must be safe. This is a potentially dangerous belief that could cause problems in the near future. In addition, given the fact that the mutual fund industry participants (outside of mutual funds managed by insurance companies) are governed by provincial regulators, many investors may believe that somehow their best interests are being looked out for. This, however, may not be the case.

There is little doubt that a significant percentage of the assets put into equity mutual funds in the last couple of years has come from money formerly invested in fixed income instruments. In late 1996, one estimate had roughly a billion dollars a day coming due in GICs. With interest rates at their lowest level in 30 years, much of this money was undoubtedly looking for a better home. With all the positive rates of returns in recent years seen in equity mutual funds, the decision of where to put this available money seemed quite easy. On this note, some individuals in the popular financial media have made statements to the effect that GICs, CSBs and bonds are "for losers." "Nobody makes money by staying in bonds" claim some. Recent bond performances are often compared to the stock market and equity mutual fund performances. Such an analysis is perhaps a little too simplistic, and may in fact end up being quite misleading.

While equities represent ownership in a particular company or corporation, bonds represent a portion of the loans or financing of the issuing company or government. Because, in most cases, bonds are a loan, they have no participation in the growth of the company (the exception being convertible bonds, where the holder has the right, over a fixed period of time, to convert the bonds into common shares at a predetermined price). As a result, bonds have a limited upside. The two most important factors that bond purchasers must be aware of are the credit quality of the issuing company or government and the expected future direction of interest rates.

The implied condition, when a bond is purchased, is that a fixed payment of interest will be received (most often on a semi-annual basis) and that the bond issuer will still be in business years down the road when the time comes to pay back the principal. Surprisingly enough, over the course of history, corporate bonds have had a much better safety record than government debt. In today's bond markets, there are several agencies that review debt issued by governments and corporations and rate them on scales based upon the issuer's financial health and ability to service the debt.

While many purchasers of bonds or fixed income products generally buy with the intent of locking in a yield and holding the investment to the maturity date, others may buy to profit from the bond's upward price movement in relation to interest rate fluctuations. When interest rates drop, the face value of the bond rises, thus reflecting what the market will pay for a bond with a fixed maturity and coupon. The opposite occurs when interest rates rise, and bond prices drop. Depending on how long the bond has until maturity, changes in interest rates will have a major impact on the bond's volatility. The longer the bond's term to maturity, the more sensitive its price is to interest rate movements.

From the statistics relating bond to equity performance, it is apparent that equities have a superior long-term growth rate compared with bonds. This is the expected norm for a capitalist country. Equity investors participate in the economy's growth and can be rewarded for assuming greater risk than the bondholder.

The problem with the chart below is that it really only gives the long-term record of the stocks that have survived. The results could be totally different depending on how an individual actually chose to invest. Some may have done better, some

REAL RETURNS

	Bonds	Stocks
1930–1939	7.3	2.69
1940–1949	-0.15	4.58
1950–1959	-1.18	13.17
1960–1969	1.51	7.35
1970–1979	-0.07	2.85
1980–1989	6.99	6.05
1990–1995	10.94	8.94
Average 1930–1995	3.05	6.33*

*Note: Include dividends reinvested
  Average dividend yields for Canadian equities 4.3% (currently 1.6%)

Current Real Return Bonds – 4.0%

may have fared worse. As for the bond track record, the actual make-up of a bond portfolio held by any individual could also vary dramatically and thus produce a very different longer-term performance. In addition, the actual buying and selling of bonds at different times, when rates were either high or low, could equally have a tremendous impact on the overall rate of return achieved.

From the chart above it is quite clear that during the 15-year period ending in 1995, investors who held bonds did substantially better than if they had been in equities. In fact the difference is quite dramatic. This may come as a surprise to many investors. The rate of return required by equity holders over this time to catch up to bond holders is significant. These equity numbers do not take into account any management fees that fundholders would have had to pay, hence dropping the yield lower still.

Of course there are numerous periods when equities have enjoyed tremendous performance as compared with the returns on bonds. The bottom line is that it is virtually impossible to predict when the periods of performance of one asset class over the other will occur, which gives rise to the need for diversification (and a long-term investment horizon). No investor wants to miss the periods of time during which either stocks or bonds have their greatest percentage moves.

Interest Rate Considerations

It is quite possible for investors to make capital gains on the purchase of bonds. Unlike GICs or Canada Savings Bonds, government or corporate bonds generally have a fairly liquid market (even on smaller purchases) and bonds may be sold if the prices have moved up in a falling interest rate market. There have been at least two periods in the 1990s where interest rates have dropped considerably, rewarding those who had purchased longer-term bonds when rates were higher. On the other hand, if an individual purchases a bond and rates rise because the economy is strong, and higher inflation is present, (bond purchasers will demand a higher yield to offset the decline in real yield resulting from inflation), the face value of the bond will decrease but the purchaser, however, can hold the bond to maturity and still be guaranteed the rate of return that was given on purchase. Strip coupons, the individual interest coupons taken from a bond and sold separately to investors, offer even greater leverage on interest rate fluctuations, as less money is needed for purchase. These coupons

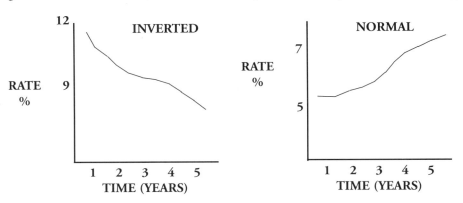

are bought at a discount to face value (like a treasury bill) and the investor collects the interest upon maturity.

Predicting interest rate movements, as mentioned earlier, is very difficult to do. One strategy for purchasing bonds is to purchase longer-term bonds when the interest yield curve is inverted (see the graph on the previous page).

Normally, the further you move out along the yield curve, the higher the interest rates will be. This makes sense in that the longer you put money in a debt instrument, the greater the risk of rises in rates, changes in government, inflation, war, etc. So, in order to take this risk, investors must be rewarded with a higher rate of interest.

In general, the central bank of a country can control short-term interest rates by easing and tightening the money supply and altering interest rates on treasury bills and overnight loans. The longer-term interest rates are affected by the market as investors decide each day what rate is appropriate for a given time period. There are buyers and sellers of debt instruments and the price is entirely determined by the considerations of supply and demand.

An inverted yield curve is the result of central bank action, choking off the money supply and raising short-term interest rates. This course of action is usually taken to slow down a strong economy and prevent undesirable inflation. Since the Second World War, a recession has always followed an inverted yield curve in the U.S. During a recession, short-term interest rates are again lowered to try to stimulate the economy (when interest rates are lower, money is cheaper to borrow, which aids economic expansion) and the whole economic cycle begins again (this is an over-simplified explanation). The reason that long-term bonds do not have higher rates

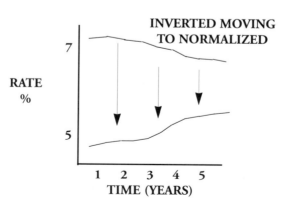

than short-term instruments in an inverted yield curve is that the market is ultimately anticipating that the economy, along with inflation, will slow, and rates will drop again, thereby providing a good real rate of return. When the inverted yield curve becomes normalized again, both the shorter-term and longer-term rates usually move down (see the previous graph).

It is at this point that long bond purchasing provides its best returns. This may not be as easy as it may appear. Until this point, both short-term and long-term rates have been rising. It becomes psychologically difficult to buy longer bonds, because these interest rate rises could continue for quite a while. However, it can be a lot easier if one approaches the purchase as a long-term potential "hold". (This philosophy is often used in RRSPs, where the use of the money in the short term is not necessary, so one can just buy and hold).

Foreign Bonds

The above description of the price behaviour of bonds holds true for foreign bonds. However, holding foreign bonds does add the variable of a foreign currency (with its own fluctuations) to the mix, as well as the effects of an economy or economies that may be at a different point in the economic cycle. Foreign bonds can provide an added component of diversification by allowing investors to hold assets outside of their country's currency. The currency component of the bond will in many cases be more volatile than the bond price fluctuations caused by interest rate movement. For more on foreign currency considerations, see the Foreign Bonds section in Chapter 12.

Key Points

- Different **asset classes** perform **differently** over any particular period of time

- It is safe to say that **equities** are likely to **outperform bonds** over the **long term** (but **timing** is everything)

- Owning a **well-diversified portfolio** containing some **real estate**, **gold**, **equities** and **bonds** is a good strategy for increasing long-term appreciation while minimizing overall portfolio volatility

Chapter 12

Should You Buy Bonds Yourself, or Invest in Bond Mutual Funds?

This question usually arises when an investor is considering the matter of how to participate in the fixed income or bond market. There are certain benefits and drawbacks to either approach and investors should decide which method of investing is best suited to their particular needs.

In This Chapter:

- **Professional Management vs. Do-It-Yourself**

- **Foreign Bonds**

- **Real Return Bonds**

- **Key Points**

Professional Management vs. Do-It-Yourself

Bond funds provide professional money management. Having a professional manager working full-time can add real value in a number of ways for the bond fund shareholder. First, because of the size of purchases and sales by the fund, better yields can be obtained as compared with the "do-it-yourself" approach. A good manager may also be able to take advantage of pricing inconsistencies within the bond market and increase the fund's overall yield without increasing the amount of risk taken. In terms of managing the bond portfolio, it may be fair to assume that the fund manager's skill and experience may add significant value when attempting to time the market and to realize capital gains on bond price movements.

There are also some compelling reasons for (and advantages to) investors managing their portfolios themselves. Because management fees are charged on bond funds (in the 0.5 to 1.75% range), the individual who invests independently starts with an advantage. The higher price paid by the individual investor when buying bonds may not be enough to warrant the bond fund option with its annual management fee. (For example, an individual who invests $50,000 in a 20-year bond at 7% would end up with $193,484. The same bond, held in a bond fund with a 1.7% management fee would have $139,127, for a difference of $54,357.) It may make more sense to use a bond fund, however, if you're planning on frequent transactions, in which case the bond price differential may make doing it yourself far more costly. If you're planning on more of a "buy and hold" strategy, and feel comfortable in your own knowledge of the subject, then it may be advisable to do it yourself. It is often possible for investors to purchase government and corporate bonds on new issues, which gets them the bond at the same price as large institutional investors. An account at a full service or discount brokerage gives the investor access to these new bond offerings.

Another benefit to self management is the fact that investors can realize capital gains or losses on bonds at their own discretion. When you've invested in a bond fund, the fund manager decides when to buy and sell bonds and the gains or losses on these transactions will affect your tax situation. When you own the bonds outright, there is a great deal more flexibility available concerning when and how to realize the gains based on your own tax situation. For example, the individual who has a capital loss on one of his or her bonds may choose to realize it by selling, and may then offset this loss with a taxable capital gain realized earlier in the year on a stock disposition. (This benefit does not apply to RRSP investments as all transactions within an RRSP are tax-free until the money is taken out.)

Foreign Bonds

For individual investors, foreign bond funds are in most cases the preferred route to investing in foreign bonds. Most purchases of bonds in the European or offshore markets require a minimum purchase amount (usually anywhere from $10,000 up) and on smaller purchases the spread between the bid and the ask can be quite large. (I have experienced this large spread situation many times when buying foreign bonds for clients — it is quite wide for smaller purchases). Foreign bond funds offer diversification with small amounts of money and have experienced money managers that will in most instances have a better knowledge and understanding of foreign bond markets than the individual investor. In fact, many North American mutual funds will hire foreign bond fund managers to manage their funds, using managers who are actually residing in, or have offices in, the area in which the bond fund invests. This is a logical step in trying to achieve the best performance possible for fundholders and can be a good selling and marketing point for the fund company.

When investing in foreign bond funds it is important to establish whether or not the fund manager has the option of using derivatives to hedge the portfolio against currency fluctuations. Many investors choose foreign bond funds for the currency diversification that those funds provide. The fund manager, however, may use derivatives to take away the currency risk that the investor may be seeking. The manager may do this through derivatives (buying calls or futures on the Canadian dollar) to offset the potential losses of the foreign bond fund holdings in Canadian dollar terms. These derivatives are not cheap and they can significantly reduce the portfolio's rate of return. A fund manager of a foreign bond fund miscalled the direction of the Canadian dollar a few years ago (thinking it would rise against European currencies) and bought calls on the Canadian dollar. The foreign currencies rose against the Canadian dollar and the fund consequently showed very little appreciation because of the high cost of purchasing the Canadian dollar calls. It was particularly frustrating for investors who thought they were properly diversified and purchased the fund under the expectation that the Canadian dollar would depreciate, only to find out that the fund manager was able (as stated in the prospectus) to hedge the foreign bond position. As this situation shows, the importance of reading the prospectus cannot be emphasized enough.

Real Return Bonds

Back in the early 1990s, the federal government issued the first real return bonds, which guaranteed a fixed rate of return above inflation. The bond was priced at par (100) and provided a 4.25% coupon over 30 years plus the monthly percentage rise in the value of the CPI (consumer price index). These bonds were created with the institutional and pension fund market in mind, but their popularity has spilled over somewhat into the retail market.

The bonds do not behave like regular bonds in that rises or falls in interest rates may not affect the price of the bond. The price of these bonds, which has been as high as $120, and just below $90 on the low end, generally moves in anticipation of inflation. If inflation is rising, it is quite possible that investors may be willing to pay a higher price for the bond (a lower guaranteed rate above inflation). With low inflation it is likely that the bond will decrease in price (a higher guaranteed rate above inflation). The CPI is calculated monthly and is tacked on to the value of the bond.

At its lowest price, the real return bond was yielding approximately 5% above inflation. Compare this return to what Canadian equities have returned above inflation since 1950 (i.e. 6%), and this is a very good rate of return with a very low risk factor. The bond does not have management fees (unlike an equity fund) and it is entirely possible that this bond, even at par (4.25% above inflation), could easily outperform most equities or equity mutual funds. Surprisingly, there is now a fund that invests almost entirely in real return bonds. It is probably much easier for the investor to buy the bonds than to pay someone to actively manage them.

This product is ideally suited for RRSP investment where all of the gain can grow tax-free. For younger RRSP buyers it is possible to purchase these bonds and calculate exactly what your future purchasing power will be in terms of today's dollars. For example, a person with $40,000 in his RRSP today (1997) can purchase a real return bond at par (the price will fluctuate) with a maturity of December 2021, hold the bond until maturity, and know that the $40,000 will be $110,897 in today's dollars. This can reduce much of the risk involved with long-term investing (and there is a lot of risk) without sacrificing too much of the potential yield.

These real return bonds have also been "stripped," meaning that the interest coupons have been taken from the bonds and sold separately, thereby enabling investors to purchase dates of real return maturities of their liking. You can purchase these strips with maturities ranging anywhere from six months to thirty years.

The U.S. recently issued a real return bond and priced it with a 3.375% rate over inflation over 10 years. Britain and Australia have also had real return bonds for some years. With the U.S. getting into the game, it is quite likely that a great deal more interest will be shown in these bonds in the future. Currently, however, very few individuals or brokers are even aware of this product, which may mean that there are some real opportunities for gain in this area.

Key Points

- **Bond funds** provide **professional management** and have the benefit of **institutional pricing** when the bonds are bought and sold.

- It is nevertheless possible for **individual investors** to obtain just as good or a potentially better rate of return by **buying bonds themselves** and **avoiding the management fees** that bond funds charge.

- **Foreign bond funds** are the preferred method of owning bonds denominated in **foreign currencies** (in most cases).

- Government of Canada **real return bonds** and **strip coupons** are a unique way of **hedging** your investment against **inflation** over both the short and long term.

Chapter 13

Tricks of the Trade

Managing money is a serious business. Well-educated men and women are paid very handsomely for the skills they possess and the often stressful conditions under which they work. While the goal of fund managers is to achieve the best rate of return for their shareholders, their success or failure is more often than not measured on short-term performance numbers. Fund companies that have shown attractive long-term performance numbers have done so largely because of the quality of their management, their portfolio managers, their research and most importantly, their ability to survive and thrive through periods of economic change and stock market volatility.

On the other side of the coin, many funds have disappeared over the years. Furthermore, of the thousands of funds available in today's market, many are relative newcomers and thus have a very short track record.

In This Chapter:

- **Short Term View —
  The Vicious Cycle**

- **Momentum Players —
  Catch the Wave**

- **Private Placements —
  Stocks at a Great Price**

- **Window Dressing**

- **Short Squeezes —
  Call In the Paper**

- **"Rat Trading" —
  What Funds Get What**

- **Key Points**

Short Term View—The Vicious Cycle

Given the competitiveness of the mutual fund industry, managing money for the best short-term rate of return is a fact of life. If one examines this statement closely, it is not difficult to understand why.

The Money Management Game

By their very nature, equity markets react immediately to the set of quarterly profit numbers (every three months) that a company releases to the public. While stock prices generally anticipate longer-term future earnings, the prospects for a company's future success are often determined by the most recently-presented quarterly earnings and the pronouncements of the Wall Street analysts as to what it all means. There can often be huge price swings on stocks, both before and after these earnings releases, that can substantially affect the value of mutual funds that hold shares in these companies. It can be very difficult for a fund manager to take a longer-term view to investing when there can be so much volatility in the shorter term. One or two quarters of sub-standard performance can really hurt a fund's perception in the eyes of the investing public.

The aforementioned situation may appear to be a foolish or self-defeating approach to investing considering that in reality, fund buyers and managers should really be concentrating on the longer-term picture. Unfortunately, it has become a vicious cycle — in the intense competition for the public's fund money, fund companies often advertise shorter-term track record performance. This is in fact necessary because many of them do not have a longer-term record. As a result, many fund managers are forced into this game, managing money in a way that may not be ideally suited for the longer term, and trying to keep up with the next guy's results.

Trying to predict or anticipate short-term price movements is a difficult task. In hot markets like the present North American equity markets, this focus on the short-term performance of stocks (particularly in the hi-tech sector) has taken on a casino-like appearance. With all of the money that has moved into mutual funds in recent years, and the large number of company stock buybacks (many companies have gone into the markets and actively bought their own shares, effectively reducing the number of shares outstanding), there has been a lot of money chasing fewer shares. There has also been a proliferation of IPOs (initial public offerings), which has offset, to some extent, the number of share buybacks. Mutual fund purchases have consistently outpaced fund redemptions by a huge margin for the better part of the 1990s, which has added fuel to the buy side of many publicly traded companies. Even stocks with questionable growth prospects, shoddy accounting and outright ridiculously high price and dividend ratios have benefitted from the large amounts of money invested by fund managers.

Momentum Players – Catch the Wave

In recent years, the popularity of buying stocks based on momentum (or on a technical basis) has grown tremendously. The fund managers who subscribe to this style of money management do not place much emphasis on the underlying fundamentals of the company, rather they focus on the trading patterns (price and volume) of the stock. While the "tape" can perhaps tell you what may happen to a stock price in the shorter term, it tells you very little about how the company will do in the long term. In defence of investors and fund managers who do use this technique, success is ultimately measured by the share price at the end of each day. If this style of money managing is producing acceptable results over a given period of time, then nobody should have any qualms about it.

One should be clearly aware, however, of the risks involved with this particular investment philosophy. At any given time, the fundholder may own a basket of stocks that could potentially have very little fundamental value and that may be held simply because their share price fits a particular pattern of buying. Hi-tech stocks seems to be an area that momentum players really like. Companies with huge price/earnings multiples that discount wildly optimistic sales and profit numbers well into the future with products that could become obsolete in a number of hours seem to be quite popular with momentum players. In fact, many companies in this sector have no earnings at all, and yet they trade with market capitalizations in the billions of dollars. Fred Hickey, a newsletter writer who follows this sector, claims that 50% of the hi-tech stocks he followed ten years ago are now gone. It is quite possible that the same fate may be awaiting the current hi-tech industry darlings (including, of course, those that are held in mutual funds).

The problem with momentum investing is that the same momentum that took the stock up could be reversed in an equally powerful downswing. In fact, stocks that trade at excessive multiples today could rapidly trade at excessive discounts if the sentiment changes to severe pessimism (which it is quite capable of doing). This situation could be further exacerbated by a large amount of fund redemption orders as the market craters. In such a situation, fund managers would be forced to sell even more stock into a falling market. The question to ask is: "Who are these momentum players going to sell their shares to when the momentum changes?" This style of investing may be compared to a game of musical chairs. The loser is the fund or individual who holds these stocks when the music stops.

While this situation is more prevalent in the U.S. equity markets, the overall potential fall-out could definitely spill over into Canadian markets. Stocks that do not have reasonable fundamentals or earnings could be punished if a frothy market turns bad.

One of the possible reasons behind the momentum investing phenomenon could be the very real difficulty in finding companies in today's market that offer real value. An organization called "IQ Trends" in La Jolla, California, tracks companies and attempts to identify those which are undervalued using a number of different indicators. This service, first started in 1966, has identified the lowest percentage of undervalued stocks in its 30-year history, with just nine companies or 2% of the total followed[1]. The problem is that fund managers who have large sums of dollars to invest find it very difficult to sit on the sidelines waiting for good values to appear when many other managers are playing a game (momentum investing) and racking up great returns.

Private Placements – Stocks at a Great Price

The number of private placements that have been done in the last few years is phenomenal. The corporate finance departments at most brokerage firms are running at full capacity putting together investment products designed for the retail customer (royalty income trusts, limited partnerships, bank split share issues, etc.). They are taking many companies public and raising money for junior oil and gas and mining companies for exploration purposes, although the mining sector may have slowed lately with the Bre-X fraud and the declining price of gold bullion. In a bull market, the corporate finance department is a major profit centre and most deals have a receptive market that will absorb them quickly. Unfortunately, a strong and successful initial public offering (IPO) market has often been a sign that the market is at or near a top.

As fund managers look for investments to purchase for their shareholders' portfolios, the private placement, which in many cases is a block of stock priced below the current market price at which the stock is trading, can be a very attractive investment.

The benefits of doing private placements are that the fund acquires stock very cheaply (well below the current stock price), and the fund shows a gain almost instantly on the value of the shares. In many of today's deals, fund managers are taking stock in smaller oil and gas or mining shares which have very little real liquidity. As a result, after the placement has been done, not much buying is needed to move the stock higher because the original float of shares was small to begin with, and the fund that has taken the private placement has agreed to hold the stock for a longer period of time (not to just "flip it" a few weeks later). In a strong market, these shares can often rise substantially, showing a large gain on paper for the fundholders. With more money flowing into mutual funds than is being redeemed, the fund manager has little to worry about as far as the lack of liquidity is concerned. If, however, the markets fall or a large number of redemption orders come in, the lack of liquidity that enabled the stock to rise spectacularly on the way up, can be just as powerful on the way down. A fund manager forced to sell stocks in an illiquid market may experience "bids drying up," meaning that there may at times be no bids (or few bids of any significant size) to sell to. The declining price of the fund can lead fundholders into more redemptions, and the game continues on the downside.

I recently had occasion to follow closely a small private placement of a gold company with prospects in Central America. The price of the placement was roughly $1.30 Canadian. The deal was to settle the following month but on the last trading day of the current month a "gray" market (an unofficial market created between traders that may evolve before a stock begins trading on an official exchange) was created and 2000 shares traded at $1.80 Canadian. Upon asking why the gray market had been set up, the answer given by the underwriter (quite candidly) was that it gave the institutions who bought the stock a closing price for month end. Instantly the funds had a 50 cent gain or a 38% return on investment! Who cares if the price has very little bearing on what the funds could actually sell the shares for?

There is absolutely nothing wrong with fund managers buying private placements for the funds they manage, and often the fact that a fund is able to take down large blocks of shares for fundholders at better prices is a real benefit to shareholders. Many precious metals funds can take healthy positions in some of the more promising junior exploration companies through this method, whereas buying this amount of stock in the market would be logistically impossible (a large amount of buying would be likely to drive the price of the stock to unrealistic levels). If just one of these stocks hits the "mother lode," the fund's asset price could skyrocket. Conversely, if a fund manager has made a mistake, or the company's prospects do not pan out, getting any amount of money out of the position is unlikely.

The private placement game has recently drawn quite a bit of attention in Canada because some fund managers have bought stock positions through private placements for their personal accounts and then subsequently purchased the same stock (at a higher price) for the fund that they are managing. This is a situation that is currently being addressed by the mutual fund industry, as the potential conflict of interest in this procedure is self-evident. It is difficult or impossible to determine whether the managers' intentions are good in such situations, or if these situations should be allowed. Nevertheless, the fund companies themselves do realize that the perception it creates is unhealthy. In response to this problem, some fund companies have forbidden their managers to buy stocks for their own personal accounts while they are managing a fund. While this is a somewhat extreme measure, it does go a long way towards preventing fund manager conflicts of interest.

Window Dressing

This term refers to the market actions that may take place at the end of every quarter. Window dressing is an attempt by mutual and pension fund managers to show, at the end of each quarter, quality stock holdings that have risen over the previous three months. It can be an embarrassment for a fund manager to be holding a stock that has recently fallen in price, so an attempt may be made to completely sell out of it before the fundholders can see it. In doing so, the portfolio can look a lot better on the surface in terms of the stocks that it currently holds, even though some bungling may have occurred in between statements.

Peter Lynch made some interesting comments on this subject (albeit indirectly) in his book *One Up on Wall Street*. Lynch noted that fund managers in general would tend to buy stocks of the ilk of IBM and General Motors, because a poor investment in these would be a lot easier to explain to a fund's board of directors and its fundholders than buying some silly sounding growth company that fizzled out. In a sense, perception is a major factor involved in stock selection, which relates to the practice of window dressing each quarter. How many fund managers take part in this practice? It is hard to say — suffice it to say that some portfolios may be a bit misleading at quarter's end.

Another component of window dressing may be the sharp or subtle price rises that certain stocks experience at the end of every quarter. Obviously the higher the share prices that are held in a portfolio, the better the fund performance and the better the fund manager looks. It may take very little buying by the fund manager to nudge stocks up at the end of a fund's quarterly reporting period. Again, how much of this may happen is difficult to know. I recall one particular mutual fund (which happened to be very heavily weighted in a specific sector) that had almost every stock in the portfolio go up quite significantly on the last trading day of the year. The fund's performance for that one day was approximately 3%. The first day of the following year, the fund's value dropped right back to where it had started. (Interestingly enough, this particular fund has since disappeared, along with its manager.)

Short Squeezes – Call In the Paper

One of the ways to get a stock price moving up quickly is to orchestrate a short squeeze with its shares.

Shorting is a term given to the practice of selling shares that you don't own on the market. The goal of short sellers is to sell stock at a high price and then buy it back when the price is lower. This form of trading is mostly done by professional traders or sophisticated investors who feel that the price of a stock is too high given its true or perceived value. To execute a short sale, you must first find someone who will lend you their share certificates. You then sell these shares in the market on the understanding that, at some time in the future, you will have to buy them back and return them to the owner.

For most publicly traded companies, shares are easy to borrow, because they are widely held by many investors, and finding someone to lend them usually only requires a telephone call. Once the stock has been borrowed and then sold, the short seller waits for the price to drop. If the stock goes down, the shares are often bought back and a gain is achieved. If the stock rises, the short seller is required to put more money (or securities) into the account to cover the unrealized loss on the account. Of course, as share prices rise, more margin is required to continue to hold the position.

When a stock is shorted, the short seller must declare at the time of sale that the stock being sold is a short. The number of shares short, or a stock's short interest, is publicly known. In the case where a certain stock has a very large short interest, a short squeeze may be orchestrated.

A short squeeze occurs when the investors or institutions that lent their stock out (often in concert together, although this is never admitted), start asking for it back from the short sellers. The short sellers may be given very little notice when asked to return the borrowed stock. If the short sellers fail to comply, they may be "bought in," meaning the brokerage firm will buy the stock back and send the short seller the bill. When a short squeeze takes place, it is not unusual to see the price of the shorted stock shoot up as short sellers pile into the market to buy back their shares. Stocks that are already grossly over priced can go up to stratospheric levels because of the underlying game that is going on.

Recently, a former employee of a major U.S. mutual fund company claimed that a daily list was given out to all the firm's money managers with the short positions on all the stocks that were in their portfolios. The purpose of this list, he claims, was to alert the managers to stocks that might be good candidates on which to run a short squeeze. A clever manager can sell a large position of his or her holding into the rising market as the short squeeze progresses, often netting the fund some very good short-term gains.

Just how often this situation occurs in the mutual fund money management scene is hard to say. It is probably more common in the funds that invest a lot of money in the hi-tech or junior mining sectors, where very volatile price swings occur and valuations on a company's real worth are very difficult to assess.

"Rat Trading" — What Funds Get What

I recently read an investment letter that warned about the practice of "rat trading," which the author claimed was a common occurrence in many mutual fund companies. "Rat trading" occurs when a fund company buys stock to be put into any of their mutual funds. The article stated that it is possible for the fund company to hold the stock that it purchased in a general trading account for a while and then distribute it to a desired mutual fund at a later date. The idea is that the fund company can see which way the price of the stock is going and then direct it to the fund that best suits its objectives. In this way the fund company can put the good purchases into its flagship fund (the fund with the best rate of return, which is also marketed the most), and put the poorer purchases into the weaker funds.

Rat trading is an illegal practice and it is very difficult to know how often it actually does occur. From speaking to fund managers and institutional salespeople about this practice, I have concluded that it doesn't happen very often, as the short-term "edge" that it gives to certain funds is small in the greater scheme of achieving superior investment returns. It is worth noting, however, because all of the fund companies do have one or two funds that underperform the averages or underperform other funds within their family of funds, so buyers should be aware that these funds may not necessarily get as much attention as the larger, more recognizable funds.

Key Points

- Many mutual funds compete for the public's money. This fact can lead fund companies to a **management approach** that only considers the **short term**.

- **Momentum investing** strategies used by some fund managers can have very **negative consequences** when a rising market peaks and begins to **turn down**.

- **Private placement** of stock in a mutual fund's portfolio can cause some very impressive **short-term gains** but **may be very illiquid** when it comes time for the fund to sell.

- **Window dressing** can disguise the happenings within a mutual fund portfolio each quarter and can, in some cases, lead to inflated **net asset values** for the fund at the **end of each quarter**.

Notes:
[1] Richard Russell, *Dow Theory Letters*, October 23, 1996, p. 3.

Chapter 14

RRSPs: Changing Policies and Foreign Content

The RRSP market for all fund companies and marketers of managed money products is huge. In fact, around 35% of all mutual fund purchases in Canada are done within RRSPs. The marketing muscle put into the selling of mutual funds for the RRSP is considerable, and is ultimately aided by the advantages that the investor receives through RRSP investment (the tax deferral of contributions to the RRSP and the tax free growth of money in the RRSP). Equity mutual funds are considered by many to be an ideal investment for the RRSP because they can often outperform fixed income products and the RRSP is generally held for a long time period, giving the holder of mutual funds within the RRSP ample time to see the benefits of holding equity investments over the long term.

Below is a chart of the RRSP contribution limits for investors over the next nine years as described in the 1996 Federal Budget.

In This Chapter:

- **Will RRSP Rules Change in the Future?**

- **The Government Frequently Changes the Rules and Regulations Concerning RRSPs**

- **RRSPs are Viewed by Some as a Financial Vehicle for the Wealthy**

- **RRSPs Could Increasingly Become a Tool for Political Ends**

- **Tax Rates May Change by the Time You Decide to Take the Money Out**

- **The Possibility of 100% Foreign Content in an RRSP**

- **The Use of Derivatives**

- **Key Points**

RRSP Contribution Limits

Year	RRSP Limit
	$
1991	11,500
1992	12,500
1993	12,500
1994	13,500
1995	14,500
1996–2003	13,500(a)
2004	14,500
2005	15,500
2006	indexed(b)

Notes

(a) The February 1995 Federal Budget reduced the contribution limit to $13,500 for 1996. The March 1996 Federal Budget froze the limit at $13,500 through 2003.

(b) After 2005, this limit will be indexed by the growth in the average wage rate in Canada.

The RRSP has generally been viewed as an effective way for individuals to save for their retirement. When contributing to an RRSP, the individual can write off the contributed amount from his or her earned income. This amount continues to grow tax-free in the RRSP, until it is removed from the RRSP. The beauty of this plan is that large gains can be made, either through the power of compound interest (in the case of fixed income investments over a long period of time) or through tax-free capital gains (in the case of equities or equity mutual funds). The end date return numbers are truly staggering when presented in relation to how early in life an individual starts contributing to an RRSP.

For example, a recent advertisement compares the total amount saved by two individuals who start saving at different times. The results, depicted in the advertisement, (see below) are an eye-opener. Note that the first individual starts saving at age 23 and stops at age 31, while the second individual saves from age 31 to age 65.

The Results of Early Contribution to an RRSP

Total at Retirement

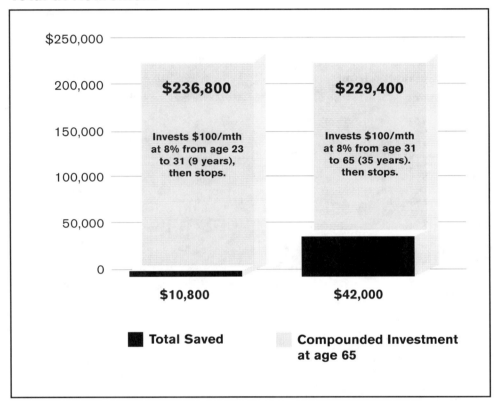

The above advertisement (from TD Bank) adequately illustrates the power of tax-free compounded growth.

Will RRSP Rules Change in the Future?

Over time, the federal government has considerably increased the amount that individuals can contribute to an RRSP (with various adjustments along the way), in an attempt to achieve a fair balance between people who have defined benefit plans and those who do not. One of the government's goals was to make people more responsible for their own retirement needs, thereby relieving the already financially overburdened and stressed federal government from many of its obligations in this area. Unfortunately, in the 1996 federal budget, the contribution limit was adjusted downwards to $13,500 for the period from 1997 to 2002, when it was previously supposed to be raised to $14,500. In addition, the required date of RRSP termination was changed from 71 to 69. (This two-year change in the age withdrawal requirement represents a huge tax grab for the government as it can now start taxing a potentially large amount of money two years earlier).

RRIF minimum payouts			
Age	% RRIFs value	Age	% RRIFs value
69	4.76	84	9.93
70	5.00	85	10.33
71	7.38	86	10.79
72	7.48	87	11.33
73	7.59	88	11.96
74	7.71	89	12.71
75	7.85	90	13.62
76	7.99	91	14.73
77	8.15	92	16.12
78	8.33	93	17.92
79	8.53	94	20.00
80	8.75	95+	20.00*
81	8.99	96+	20.00*
82	9.27	* continues at 20% until capital depleted	
83	9.58	Source: RBC Dcm. Sec's	

The recent federal government proposal to change the current retirement benefits for seniors illustrates just how much change is being considered. It is proposed that, beginning in 2001, the Old Age Security, the Guaranteed Income Supplement, the Pension Income Credit and the Age Tax Credit should be replaced by a tax-free "Senior's Benefit." If eventually adopted, this plan would eliminate all benefits for single seniors who have an income of over $52,000 a year, or for couples with a combined income of over $78,000. Effectively, this would mean that anyone taking sufficient money out of an RRSP or RRIF to push his or her income over that threshold amount of $52,000 (or $78,000 for couples), would be taxed on that money at a rate of 70%. (The seniors' benefits that are foregone by exceeding those threshold amounts cause this somewhat extreme result.) The proposal is a remarkable disincentive for an individual to save for retirement. It should be viewed as a "wake-up call" to Canadians regarding the government's future plans and how those plans will affect our retirement.

One point worth mentioning here is the tax benefit of the spousal RRSP. A married individual can contribute up to his or her maximum into the spouse's "spousal" RRSP and deduct the contribution from his or her taxable income. After three years, this money can be taken out by the spouse and taxed at his or her personal income tax rate. If this spouse is in a much lower tax bracket, or doesn't work or pay tax, the benefit can be very substantial. Also, if it is held until retirement, the income from the RRSP can be split up and received by two people instead of one, which lowers the amount of tax paid. (Couples should try to distribute RRSP or pension income evenly so both receive the same amount in retirement.)

While the RRSP may still be regarded as a good investment vehicle for most people, one must look at several different factors that can significantly reduce its benefits in years to come. Consider the following:

The Government Frequently Changes the Rules and Regulations Concerning RRSPs

Given the government's tendency to change the rules, as illustrated above, we in the investment community are often left wondering what they will do next. One rumour that circulated in recent years was that there would be a 1% yearly tax on assets held within an RRSP. This may seem unfair or unreasonable to many at first glance, but it is no different from what happened to individuals who expected to receive full Old Age Security benefits, and subsequently had them taken away.

RRSPs are Viewed by Some as a Financial Vehicle for the Wealthy

The statistics on who contributes to RRSPs, and in what amounts, reveal that many Canadians don't contribute to RRSPs. Those that do are generally from a higher net worth or socio-economic background. Articles in the media have highlighted these statistics and have, in certain instances, implied that RRSPs represent a tax break for the rich. In light of this, it may be reasonable to assume that the government may also start to think along these lines, viewing RRSP monies as its own because of the tax concessions originally given when people contributed. In reality, the RRSP is only a tax deferral, so the government could quickly change the deferral time to its liking. It would be able to justify such a move because, after all, RRSPs are "only used by the rich." (The last NDP Government in Ontario considered those families who made more than $50,000 a year to be "wealthy." This sort of classification illustrates the dangers faced by people who have worked hard to save considerable amounts of money.)

RRSPs Could Increasingly Become a Tool for Political Ends

Because the RRSP rules are set by the government, they may be changed from time to time to the benefit of some and to the detriment of others. For example, the rules were recently changed so that anyone who bought a new house could take a certain amount of money out of their RRSP to use as a down payment. ($20,000 is the maximum allowable RRSP withdrawal for a home purchase and it must be paid back to the RRSP over a 15-year period). Why this rule was brought in is debatable. Quite possibly, the government thought that buying a house could be considered a legitimate investment that would help people save for the future (there is currently no capital gain on the sale of a principal residence, which lends support to this RRSP change).

More skeptical individuals may have seen this move as a subsidy to the depressed real estate and housing sector. This rule made home buying more affordable to Canadians and thus could stimulate housing demand through greater monies being available for down payments on housing purchases. Many economists will argue that this type of incentive is the reason why recessions and depressions occur. Specifically, the tax incentives and disincentives alter the real supply and demand relationship and cause severe imbalances that can take years to reverse. For example, the real estate markets in many Canadian cities have been experiencing very difficult times following the extreme price inflations of the late 1980s. This type of RRSP incentive may do more long-term harm than good, stimulating a market that is still recovering from previous imbalances.

Tax Rates May Change by the Time You Decide to Take the Money Out

A few years back, I had a very interesting discussion with a banker who claimed that RRSPs were a poor investment. He stated that investors should pay the tax on their income now and ship the money out of the country. His reasoning was that by the time it came time to take money out of your RRSP, the taxes you will pay on it will be much higher. An offshore trust made much more sense in his mind. Without debating the offshore trust recommendation, the banker made a valid point. What the taxes will actually be when you take your money out of an RRSP is a difficult question to answer. With any luck, the tax-deferred growth within the RRSP will more than offset the potential tax liabilities when you withdraw your money. But who knows? Will RRSPs still be around 20 years from now?

Non-Canadian Investing

Independent Markets with Different Risk/Return Patterns
Risk/Return Performance Comparison
10 Years Ending 12/31/94

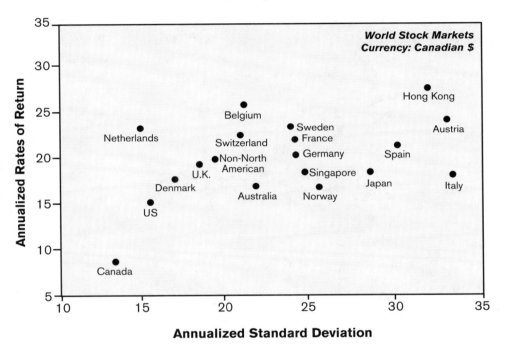

The above graph shows what an increase in risk taken by a Canadian investor would return through investing in foreign markets based on returns over a 10 year period ending December 31, 1994.

Increasing the Foreign Content of Your RRSP

The current RRSP rules allow for a 20% holding of foreign property within an RRSP. As a result, most Canadian equity funds will stay at or under this limit, so that the fund will be entirely RRSP-eligible. Despite the fact that these funds may have 20% foreign content, they are viewed entirely as Canadian content. Therefore, one could theoretically have up to 36% foreign content within an RRSP by investing 20% of the money in an international fund for foreign content, and the other 80% in a

Canadian equity fund that holds 20% foreign equities. Considering that the Canadian equity market makes up roughly 2.7% of world equity values, maximizing foreign holdings makes sense for greater diversification and asset appreciation potential.

Recent discussions held in the Senate on this subject suggest that changes may be made to the foreign content restrictions on RRSPs, that would allow for a greater usage of foreign holdings within these vehicles. What is eventually decided on this subject should be of great interest to investors.

While the benefits of allowing Canadians greater freedom of choice for their RRSP are self-evident, it should be considered that that is not necessarily something that the Canadian government would like to see. In recent years, the federal government and most of the provinces have increasingly become dependent upon foreigners for purchasing new debt issues. One of the features that has made Canadian bonds attractive to foreigners is that there is no withholding tax on the interest earned. Many foreign institutions and individuals (who in many instances live or operate in a much more favourable tax environment) can achieve fairly attractive rates of return in real terms and are also provided with good liquidity should they wish to sell at a future date. This practice is costly for the government — if domestic demand was able to absorb the new debt issues, taxes could be extracted on a large amount of the interest that is paid out. With foreign buying, this tax is forfeited. So there is a definite incentive for the government to finance its debt domestically. One way to do that is to reduce the allowable amount of foreign content within RRSPs. If a large part of newer government debt was purchased in RRSPs, taxes would still be extracted, but on a deferred basis (when any funds were withdrawn). Having a greater amount of its debt held domestically could also give the government greater freedom in terms of its monetary policy, although this point is debatable.

There are arguments currently being put forth that foreign bond and debt holders have too much power in terms of forcing governments whose bonds they own to behave in a certain way, i.e., being more fiscally responsible. Voters may complain that politicians pay too much attention to these interests, while neglecting policies that are needed domestically and are in its citizens best interests. This is a very difficult situation because, in a real sense, the foreign bond holders have financed the country's overspending and therefore have a right to exert pressure on the government to ensure the return of principal and interest. Many people, however, do not see it this way and are strongly opposed to the thought of having others control how their government or their society operates.

Taking this argument one step further, countries that do run into financial problems have often applied currency controls, which effectively prohibit their citizens from placing or investing their money outside the country. In this kind of situation it is common to see the value of the currency debased, while the country's debts and deficits are inflated away. This is a very undesirable circumstance, in which nobody is spared from the drop in the standard of living. (This situation highlights the benefit of offshore trusts where investment flexibility can still be maintained.)

The above scenario is intended to alert the investor to the underlying meaning behind policy changes made by governments to investment legislation. As a result, investors should take the time to interpret any new or forthcoming RRSP legislation so as to best protect their wealth and assets from governments that are desperately seeking new sources of income.

The Possibility of 100% Foreign Content in an RRSP

Very few individuals are aware that it is in fact possible to eliminate the Canadian dollar exposure of assets within an RRSP.

Because Canada is a member of many international organizations, debt issued by these entities is considered Canadian for RRSP purposes. For example, the World Bank and the International Bank for Reconstruction and Development, two organizations to which Canada belongs, issue many bonds in many different currencies. An individual could buy a World Bank bond denominated in Swiss Francs, put the bond in his or her RRSP, and effectively divest him or herself of any Canadian dollar exposure. These bonds can in many cases be bought through banks or brokerage houses (for purchases of $10,000 Canadian and up) and put in self-directed RRSPs.

In recent years, some mutual fund companies have created funds that are 100% RRSP-eligible, yet track or mimic foreign equity and bond markets. Using the same principle mentioned above, certain fund companies will buy a basket of different bonds issued by international organizations of which Canada is a member. The manager will diversify the portfolio in terms of currency and duration of the bonds, yet it will all be 100% Canadian content. Unlike domestic bond funds, a large part of the return on an international bond fund can come from fluctuations on the different currencies of the bonds held within the funds. The fund manager in this situation must not only try to gauge which way interest rates may head in all the different countries in which currency exposure is held, but also try to accurately forecast which way the currencies will go relative to one another. As a result, the fund may be weighted in different proportions depending on the manager's outlook.

The Use of Derivatives

Some of the newer funds, capitalizing on the desire of many individuals to diversify a large part of their RRSPs into foreign equity markets, have been able to achieve this goal through the use of derivatives. Derivatives allow the owner to participate in a leveraged way in the market moves of a variety of market indexes in most major world exchanges. In most cases the fund will meet the RRSP eligibility requirement by keeping 80% of the fund's money in Canadian bonds or treasury bills. With the other 20%, a number of different options or futures will be purchased in a mix that will reflect the performance of the indexes as if the full 100% of the money in the fund were invested. For example, if one of the desired markets to invest in was Japan, the fund manager might buy calls or futures on the Nikkei index. Assuming, for simplicity's sake, this was the only market desired, on a $10 initial fund value, $2 would be used for call or future purchases. If the Nikkei index rose 10%, (assuming the goal of the fund is to mimic as closely as possible the desired market) the fund value should be $11. Therefore the fund manager would have to buy enough calls or futures with the initial $2 to earn $1 (or a 50% gain) on a market rise of 10%. This is quite possible because of the nature and use of leverage. It is important to note that these types of funds are managed so that fundholders will never lose more than they put in (as opposed to hedge funds where you can be liable for losses greater than the money initially invested — see Chapter 15). For example, if the desired index dropped 90%, the fund example above would drop from $10 to $1, mimicking the index. In many of these types of funds, the manager will take this sort of position on a wide variety of market indexes, overweighting in some, and underweighting in others, to create a well-diversified RRSP-eligible international equity mutual fund.

While this example is simplified, it does give a rough idea of what kinds of products are available today for investors who want a lot of variety and flexibility in the investments that they put into their RRSPs. In terms of the variety of available products, the mutual fund industry has been very innovative and receptive to the wants, needs and demands of the investing public.

Key Points

- The **tax deferral** and **tax-free growth** benefits of **RRSPs** make them a good way of saving for retirement.

- **RRSP rules** are **likely to change** in the future (probably to the detriment of investors).

- **Increasing** the **foreign content** of your **RRSP** (which can be done in many ways) can help to improve your **long-term investment performance** through greater **diversification**.

Chapter 15

Index Funds, Hedge Funds, Funds of Funds and Derivatives

Index Funds

Given the likelihood of most mutual funds underperforming the major market indexes, index funds are a popular means of insuring that the investor at least comes close to achieving similar rates of return to the general indexes. Index funds can either hold shares in all the companies that make up a particular index, or they can hold futures or derivatives that will mimic the performance of a particular index. The distinction is of critical importance. The index fund that holds the individual stocks will receive the dividends paid by the stocks, whereas index funds made up of derivatives and options will not. Interestingly, the S&P 500, since 1790, has averaged 3.28% annual growth without the dividend. For the first time in history, the dividend yield on the S&P 500 (currently at 1.61%) is lower than many of the annual management fees charged on equity mutual funds.

Because of management fees and switching charges (when a stock is either added to or dropped from the index) it is virtually impossible to achieve the same return as the actual index. It is possible, however, to come close.

When purchasing an index fund, a careful examination of the charges is essential. Not all index funds will have the same costs associated with trying to mimic a given market.

In fact, in certain instances these costs have caused certain index funds to underperform their desired index by more than 2%. This type of shortfall will affect longer-term performance numbers enough to cause one to question whether the whole exercise is even worthwhile. Unfortunately, the prospectus cannot accurately predict costs other than the management fee, so past charges should be looked at and questioned to try to establish a realistic cost against future performance.

In the last several years, some federal agencies of the Government of Canada, as well as some banks and trust companies, have issued bonds and GICs that guarantee a rate of return matching a wide variety of domestic and foreign stock market indexes. The terms of each of these issues vary considerably (i.e., some pay 125% of the market performance whereas others may pay 100%). The nice part about these products is that they guarantee the return of the principal investment on the maturity date. The rate of return is paid at the end in most cases, and it is treated as interest income. (Most of these products have no foreign currency risks. The percentage rate of return of the index is paid in Canadian dollars.) These products have their benefits and should be considered when creating an investment portfolio. One thing to remember, however, is that these products do not pay the dividend income that would be paid if you actually owned the stocks in the index. When looking at the historical data, it is important to remember how large a part dividend income (which the investor forgoes in choosing these products) plays in long-term investment performance.

One index that deserves mention is the TSE 35 or "TIPS" index. The TIPS holds a basket of stocks that represent the stocks that make up the TSE 35 index. Established by the Toronto Stock Exchange (TSE), this product trades on the TSE and charges no management fee. Instead, investors are paid the dividends earned 90 days after theoretical payment to the fund. As a result, this index mimics very closely the TSE 35 performance. This has no effect on current purchasers of this product.

It should be noted that many mutual funds do outperform index funds in a declining market, since the cash in the mutual funds cushions the blow (in most cases, mutual funds will have at least a small amount of cash at hand).

Hedge Funds

A hedge fund or hedge account, by definition, is an account that is technically market neutral, but that does (through the use of leverage or derivatives) profit from market volatility. For example, one of the most popular hedge strategies involves the use of convertible bonds and common shares. It is sometimes possible through price discrepancies between a company's convertible debentures (or bonds), and its common shares, to profit, with very little risk, by taking a long position in the bonds and at the same time shorting the equivalent dollar amount of common shares. Without going into too much detail, the position can be market neutral from the standpoint that the same number of shares shorted is also owned long through the convertibility of the bond into common shares. Because the convertible debenture pays interest and usually will not drop as much as the common shares (if the common shares drop a lot, the interest payable on the bond will prevent it from dropping as much), profits can be made on these pricing differences when market fluctuations take place.

The same hedge strategy can be adjusted to take a bullish or bearish weighting: specifically, the hedge can be adjusted to be more profitable if the market goes in the direction desired by the individual implementing the strategy. Of course, there is more downside risk to the investor if the opposite occurs. Hedged positions have the ability to achieve excellent rates of return with a much lower risk potential than holding stocks outright.

Hedge funds or hedge accounts will monitor market conditions to try to find pricing discrepancies in many different types of investment products. Unfortunately, the term "hedge fund" is often misused when describing many of the more aggressive mutual funds in today's market. This situation was pointed out to me by Scott Leckie (Senior Vice-President of MMI Group in Toronto). Many of the funds that use derivatives to take extremely speculative positions in the equity or currency markets are characterized as hedge funds. Most of the positions that are taken in these funds have no real "hedge" component to them at all. As a result, we sometimes hear about mutual funds that are forced to be wound up because all of the equity in the fund has disappeared. This often occurs after a big swing or strong rally in a particular market. For example, a few years back a number of these so-called hedge funds disintegrated after a strong stock market rally because many of them had taken very large short positions in shares that just kept going up. This is not permitted in Canada as Canadian mutual funds cannot use leverage.

Hedge accounts are different from hedge funds in that the individual owns or has purchased a specific hedge position in his or her own account (as opposed to being in a pooled fund). There are individual brokers that do this type of account for investors, with minimum amounts required generally being in the range of $25,000 and up. A properly implemented hedge account can offer very high rates of return with minimal amounts of risk. Many brokerage firms offer convertible debenture booklets with all of the relevant information regarding all current outstanding convertible debentures. They will often offer some hedging strategy ideas.

Funds of Funds

Recently, the funds of funds concept has again become popular. Funds of funds are mutual funds that buy other mutual funds. The idea is that the manager goes out and buys other mutual funds, attempting to add value for his shareholders through skilful selection and asset weighting of these funds. In essence, the fund manager, instead of investing the monies directly into the desired stocks or markets, chooses other funds and managers to invest in.

The logic behind this practice is the belief that the manager of the fund of funds will be better able to select and balance a basket of mutual funds than the individual. The only problem is that another layer of fees is added. The manager of the fund of funds often will take 1% or more for his or her services. However, he or she may, through special arrangement, be able to reduce the management fees on the funds that are chosen.

Funds of funds were popular back in the late 1960s when the mutual fund industry was booming. They largely disappeared during the bear markets in the early 1970s and have only recently resurfaced. It may be argued that they are only popular when markets are strong. Most people don't mind paying management fees when the returns they are receiving are strong, but when market returns are weaker or negative, these kinds of products are increasingly difficult to justify in investors' minds. Canadian regulators have suspended the formation of any new funds of funds in recent years. (Of the investment trusts that have been issued recently, however, some do purchase other investment trusts.)

Derivatives

As mentioned earlier, financial derivatives have recently become a much larger component in the investment arena. Derivatives are designed to mimic or reproduce the price action or movements of the desired underlying equity or bond market. Some recent mutual funds have been created which employ these derivative products to allow investors to participate in many different world markets in a variety of ways. For example, to get around the foreign content restrictions of RRSPs, derivatives may be used to give a mutual fund 100% market exposure to a number of different foreign equity markets, while still being considered Canadian content (see Chapter 14).

Originally, derivatives were often used as a hedge by businesses or corporations that bought or sold products in foreign markets. The futures markets for agricultural products are a good example of hedging — farmers or growers of produce can determine the selling price of their product long before the seeds are actually planted. Because of the nature of currency markets, with their wild fluctuations, it is often necessary for businesses to "lock in" future prices or values on the currency in which they will be charging or receiving. This allows a company the ability to plan its future course, eliminating a large amount of potential risk. This hedging ability does, however, come at a cost (the premium and commission on an option, or the commission on a futures contract) but this cost is relatively small when it is compared with the amount of risk eliminated.

Of more interest to the market player or mutual fund investor are the derivatives created to mimic movement on all sorts of equities, bonds, equity indexes and bond indexes. It is interesting to note that the dollar value of what all derivatives represent today dwarfs the actual underlying value of the markets or equities that they represent. That is to say, if the dollar value of all the stocks that are listed on an index, for example, totalled $10 billion, it is quite possible that the derivatives that trade each day representing these stocks of the index may represent $200 billion worth of these stocks. Put more simply, because relatively little money is needed to buy a derivative vehicle (in many cases a $1,000 payment is needed for a derivative representing $100,000 worth of stock), investors and professional traders can buy and sell contracts back and forth that represent huge underlying assets, and the assets they represent are often much greater than the real market itself. As a result, the derivative markets can often seriously affect the underlying market, causing wild fluctuations in stock prices that really have no underlying relationship to the value of the particular shares. Computer trading models that monitor values on futures markets (futures are derivatives) and equity markets are often programmed to kick in buy or sell orders when a profit can be made on the basis of the price relationship between the two. This is known as arbitrage, and it is a game which is played constantly.

The derivative markets are of interest to the mutual fund investor, since they may be used in mutual funds. They can also help explain why prices may be so volatile in the markets in which mutual funds invest. It may be fair to say that volatility is here to stay and that its shocks are a fact of life in today's markets.

Key Points

- **Index funds** can be used to achieve the **general market returns** for many different markets. Different funds will have **different fees and costs**.

- **Hedge funds** are designed to take advantage of **pricing discrepancies** that occur in the **financial markets** and can achieve **attractive rates of return** over a **short period** with **minimal risk**.

- **Funds of funds** can **add value** for the investor but this must be weighed against the **extra layer of fees** that must be paid.

- **Derivatives** and **derivative trading** have a **large role** in **financial markets** today. **Mutual funds may use derivatives** in many ways in attempting to achieve their stated goals.

Chapter 16

Recommendations

With all the investment information currently available, it is (ironically) becoming more and more difficult to know what to do with your money. Many of the investment recommendations being offered today are quite often contradictory in nature, and some can even be blatantly wrong in many of the assumptions that they make. Keeping this in mind, a short list of time-tested and conservative basic rules is presented below. Investing doesn't have to be overly complicated (despite how convoluted some people make it) and it is possible to achieve very high real rates of return through the disciplined application of an appropriate plan.

These recommendations are specific to the mutual fund investor although in many cases they can also be applied by individuals who own common shares or who wish to pick stocks themselves.

Consider Using Dollar Cost Averaging

This strategy allows an individual to invest a given amount of money every month, or every quarter (or whatever time period is chosen) into the market. Based on the assumption that equity markets will rise over time (a reasonable assumption) the money goes into the market at both higher prices and lower prices and helps smooth out the

In This Chapter:

- **Consider Using Dollar Cost Averaging**
- **Value Averaging**
- **Constant-Ratio Investing**
- **Variable-Ratio Investing**
- **Buy Well-Established Funds**
- **Look for Low Management Expense Ratios**
- **Be Aware of How Commissions Affect Your Returns**
- **Choose Funds With Low Portfolio Turnover**
- **Mutual Fund Purchases Should Not Be Made Late in the Year**
- **Diversify Your Investments**
- **Avoid The Advertising Hype**
- **Consider A Portfolio of Index Funds, Real Return Bonds, Strip Coupons or Regular Bonds**
- **Try Not To Make Decisions Based On Your Emotions**
- **Examine the Mutual Fund Portfolio**
- **Remember That It's Your Money**
- **Consider the Benefits of Off-Shore Trusts and Corporations**
- **Additional Information**

potential risk of investing a lump sum at one specific time. As past statistics reveal, timing can be everything, and if you choose an improper purchase date it can take you years to recover.

Dollar cost averaging also helps eliminate the natural inclination to buy stocks when they are up and sell stocks when they are down. I've often heard the following comment about the stock market: "It's the only market where people buy when the merchandise is pricey and totally ignore it when there's a great firesale on." It is a fair assumption that many investors (including the professionals) are guilty of this behaviour. It is said that the markets are principally governed by two emotions, greed and fear. Greed leads one to buy more when stocks are going up (trying to hit the home run) and fear causes one to panic when prices are falling and undervalued. If you follow the dollar cost averaging principle, this self-defeating behaviour can be avoided.

Other excellent strategies along the dollar cost averaging line were presented recently in an article in the *Globe and Mail* by Gordon Powers[1]. They included:

Value Averaging

This stategy promotes the purchasing of greater dollar amounts of mutual funds when they are down and selling a predetermined amount when they reach a higher price target. In the example given in the article, the investor's strategy is to increase the value of the fund by $100 each month. Starting with $100 the first month, if in one month the fund goes up $40 (to $140), then the investor puts in $60 for the next month. If the fund drops $20 (to $80), then $120 would be needed to keep the $100 monthly average increase in line. Following three months, if the fund's value is above the desired pre-set target, then the amount above this target is sold (taking the profit) and the process continues. If the fund isn't above the target, the investor simply continues until the subsequent targets are achieved. Harvard Professor Michael Edelson, who has done a study on this technique, claims that it consistently outperformed straight dollar cost averaging over rolling five-year periods going back to 1926.

Constant-Ratio Investing

With this strategy, the investor determines the percentage balance of funds desired (i.e., 60% equity, 40% bonds). Each month the investor then contributes the same fixed amount of money in that ratio, and based on the percentage changes in value of the two asset classes after three months, the future contributions are adjusted to get back to the original 60/40 split. This strategy is a good way to reduce overall risk, and boost returns. The data tabulated by Altamira, who studied this strategy, certainly backs this up.

Variable-Ratio Investing

Although similar in structure to the constant-ratio plan, variable-ratio investing calls for an increase in the money committed to equity funds when they drop below a predetermined level, and a decrease in the purchasing of such funds when they go above a certain target. This style must use certain assumptions as to what the market will do over the coming years, and therefore its objectives require more investor interpretation when establishing the buying and selling targets (which creates more risk).

Like dollar cost averaging, these strategies preclude the emotional decision factor of when to get in and out of the market. They also force the investor to buy more when prices are down and sell more when prices are higher. If they are strictly followed, they can make a huge difference in overall rates of return.

Buy Established Funds With Longer Performance Histories

Because it is difficult to obtain long-term performance numbers for many mutual funds, it is advisable to buy funds managed by those companies that have lasted over the decades. While past performance may not help too much in predicting future performance (many will argue this point), it is realistic to assume that the fund companies that have been around for a long time have been able to do so because they have been reasonably successful. Granted, many of the fund managers at a given fund company may have changed over the years, but the company investment philosophy and practices can remain intact and perpetuate further success over time. It is quite easy to obtain the names of fund companies that have been in existence for a long time and a study of the funds offered by these companies should reveal some of the better funds and their managers.

Look for Low Management Expense Ratios

The lower the management fees and expenses, the less drag there is on portfolio performance. As discussed earlier, the year-over-year effects of having 0.5% to 1.0% additional charges on one fund over another can make a big difference to overall yields. Several studies claim that funds with lower expense ratios tend, as a group, to outperform funds with higher fees. This seems quite plausible, as the funds with the higher fees would have to consistently outperform the lower-fee funds just to stay even. It obviously doesn't make sense, however, to invest in low-fee funds if their performance over time is questionable or poor.

The purchase of closed-end funds should be considered as it is often possible to buy these funds at a large discount to net asset value. There have been times when closed-end funds have consistently traded at large discounts for a prolonged period of time, causing the managers to change the charter (with fundholder approval) and allowing the realization of the discount to be collected by making these funds open-end. It should be remembered, however, that closed-end funds can also trade at premiums. The management fees on closed-end funds are often lower than the fees on comparable open-end funds. Investors should check the numbers! (I have recently come across some closed-end funds with MERs as low as 0.15% annually!)

Be Aware of How Commissions Affect Your Returns

The commissions that you pay at the beginning or end of a mutual fund investment can affect your overall return. Fortunately, the days of the 9% front-end load are gone and the fund industry has been forced, through the creation of many no-load funds and increasing competition, to have more realistic commission charges. For the investor who wishes to do much of the fund research him or herself, buying load funds through a discount broker may be advisable. Generally, the discount brokers will charge 2% on smaller purchases and the fees will decline as the dollar value of the purchase increases. If negotiated with a full service broker, comparable commission rates are possible, as many brokers may be willing to take lower sales commissions to receive the trailer commissions generated over the period that the purchaser holds the fund. In many instances, the investor can negotiate a satisfactory fee structure with the broker or salesperson, as there are benefits for both parties in the relationship. If the client's broker is properly rewarded, the chances are good that the client will be given high consideration when the broker distributes the allotments of a good new issue or a product that is in high demand. For the broker, the relationship with the client is clearly defined and understood, and the potential for further business from the client is enhanced.

No-load funds are attractive because there is no commission to be paid either going in or going out. However, one must be careful to look at the expense ratios and track records as the money saved on the commissions may be lost on higher expenses and poor performance. There are many no-load funds that warrant investor attention today and information on these funds is easily accessible. Many of these funds can be bought through full service brokers (although they will not be heavily recommended by commissioned salesmen) because the trailer fees received by the broker or salesperson for most of these funds still make it profitable from his or her perspective.

The back-end load option may be attractive to individuals who plan on investing in mutual funds for the long term. By taking this option, there is no commission if the fund is held for a certain period (usually anywhere from 5 to 9 years), and the investor can move between different funds offered by the fund company at no extra cost. The broker or salesperson is paid the commission from the fund company (or the limited partnership established for this purpose) and is more likely to offer better service on the account because of the commitment of the client to the broker's advice and recommendations. Be careful, however, because certain funds and fund families may have a higher MER for certain funds bought with the deferred sales charge option.

Choose Funds With Low Portfolio Turnover

The number of trades done by a fund (or its turnover in stock positions) can have a tremendous impact on the amount of tax that a fundholder will pay each year. While this is not important for tax exempted investments (e.g. RRSPs), it is important for mutual funds held in regular accounts. A high turnover rate will also have additional costs in terms of the brokerage that must be paid on each transaction. A well-managed fund with high turnover may still provide better returns to the investor than the typical buy and hold strategy, but its nature gives the investor a disadvantage from the start. It is imperative that more than the track record be looked at when investing in mutual funds, because the tax consequences can make good performance numbers look much less impressive after the taxes are actually paid.

Mutual Fund Purchases Should Not Be Made Late in the Year

As mentioned earlier, the fundholder who owns the fund as of year-end must pay the taxes on the interest, dividends and capital gains accrued since the last payment period (which may go back one quarter or, more likely, to the beginning of the year). Therefore, purchases should be delayed until the following year when the fund will be priced "ex-dividend" (that is, when all the previous year's interest, dividend and capital gains have been paid out). This strategy is not necessary in tax-exempt accounts.

Diversify Your Investments

Proper diversification through investment in different assets, countries and management styles makes great sense. A little homework is all that is necessary to put together a portfolio that will weather any financial storms that may occur. Douglas Casey, in his book *Crisis Investing For the Rest of the 90's* gives the best example of diversification that I have ever seen. Casey calls it the "10 by 10" portfolio and suggests that the investor divide and invest his or her money equally between 10 totally different asset classes that have the potential to appreciate 10 times in value over the course of a business cycle. The argument is that the investor will make mistakes, but that all it takes is one or two successful picks and the investor will fare quite well. Some of the sectors recommended (when they are out of favour and trading at distressed prices) are silver, agricultural commodities, the TED spread (the interest rate differential between interest rates paid on U.S. dollars held in the U.S. and in Europe—well beyond the scope of this book!), Japanese and U.S. short sales, junior gold stocks, junior oil stocks and foreign real estate in politically distressed countries.

It is evident from the examples mentioned above that the investor needs a definite level of sophistication (and money) to implement this approach (and that it is not possible using mutual funds alone). The theory and logic behind it are, however, sound. In the same book, however, Casey also recommends a more conservative and practical portfolio strategy which can be implemented using mutual funds. The "Permanent Portfolio," developed by Harry Browne and Terry Coxon, attempts to hedge the investor against any type of economic scenario, including inflation, deflation, currency devaluation and prosperity. The six chosen asset classes are listed below:

Category	Target Percentage
Gold	20%
Silver	5%
Swiss Franc Assets	10%
Real Estate/resource stocks	15%
U.S. stocks	15%
T-Bills/T-bonds	35%

Gold is chosen to hedge against inflation or monetary crisis, silver to hedge against inflation and prosperity, Swiss francs against inflation or U.S. currency devaluation, real estate or resource stocks to hedge against inflation, U.S. stocks to benefit from prosperity and U.S. T-bills and T-bonds to hedge against deflation. The investor chooses the desired percentage in each asset class and constantly adjusts the portfolio to keep these percentages the same. This results in selling when prices are higher and buying when prices are lower. For the Canadian investor, adaptations of this portfolio are quite simple and can incorporate mutual funds for many of these asset classes. Canadian products can also be substituted into many of the sectors with great benefit to the investor. For example, Government of Canada real return bonds can be incorporated into the gold section because of their inflation hedging characteristics. (These bonds pay interest even if there is no inflation.) This kind of portfolio design makes excellent sense and does not need a lot of monitoring once it is in place.

Avoid The Advertising Hype

When certain funds are heavily marketed because of their wonderful shorter-term track records, ignore the temptation to jump in and hope that this success will continue. The odds, as the statistics will ultimately reveal, are against this performance continuing, and in fact the chances of underperformance increase (as regression back towards the mean occurs). Also, when certain fads hit the market (i.e., German funds after the wall came down, or Far East funds because of Chinese reforms), do not jump in. Chances are that the market already has a great deal of expectation built into equity prices which means that you'll probably be buying at peak prices. When disappointment follows, it is likely that the redemption of these funds will occur at the wrong time, as disgruntled investors give up all hope when the market bottoms.

Consider a Portfolio of Index Funds, Real Return Bonds, Strip Coupons or Regular Bonds

A good argument can be made for the purchase of index funds for equity exposure, real return bonds for purchasing power protection and regular bonds or strip coupons for bond market exposure. A portfolio made up of these vehicles with a proper balancing of these assets to meet the investor's risk profile can go a long way to ensuring long-term portfolio growth and asset protection. The beauty of these products is that their costs are minimal (only management fees for the index funds with possible front- or back-end commission charges) and there is not much work that needs to be done on a continuous basis (so there are fewer transaction costs). It is important to note that the bonds and strips would have commissions built into the yield on purchase and sale, but no ongoing charges for holding them. Several index funds should be chosen, along with real return bonds or strip coupons with variable maturities, as well as regular bonds or strip coupons with staggered maturities for adequate diversification. Low costs with general market performance exposure ensures that this kind of portfolio will achieve respectable and consistent returns. In the difficult world of investing, this is often viewed as a very successful strategy.

Try Not To Make Decisions Based On Your Emotions

It is a good idea to differentiate between investing and speculating. It's always interesting to watch people search for bargains or low prices when going grocery shopping or making major purchases of household or leisure items, while these same individuals will put thousands of dollars into speculative penny stocks that a neighbour or a relative has heard good things about. There is nothing wrong with speculating with your money if you can afford it, but in some ways the stock market is dangerous because it's like the race track or the casino in that it can provide a real "rush" to its participants. Whether it's horses, card games or junior stocks, however, the end result is often the same. The gambling participant usually loses. The nice part about stocks is that the game usually lasts longer.

For the individual, it is worth pointing out that the investment industry, to a large extent, caters to people's emotions. The 24-hour-a-day investment channels that continuously flash the stock prices at the bottom of the screen help create excitement by highlighting the daily fluctuations of the stock market and stock prices. The sponsors of these programs are usually the brokerage companies, who in this case, may be compared to the "house" in gambling parlance. Whether the client wins or loses, the house makes money.

Keeping this in mind, it is probably advisable that the investor who is susceptible to being swayed by the emotions in the market (and many are) should designate a fixed small amount of money for investing in the more risky smaller companies or junior stocks. Depending on how speculative the stocks are, the investor may successfully enhance his or her portfolio's overall performance numbers by hitting a winner in the junior or growth stock sector. Conversely, he or she may lose it all, but this smaller amount shouldn't be too significant in relation to the total portfolio value.

Examine the Mutual Fund Portfolio

If a mutual fund portfolio contains a lot of stocks with unrecognizable names, be careful. This is not to say that stocks without household names won't be successful investments, but an overabundance or large weighting in smaller companies can be risky. Those stocks tend to be a lot more volatile in price than the stocks of large companies with well-established earnings track records. In a strong bull market, many stocks may rise with the tide. When this happens there is often a tendency on the part of money managers to take more risk by buying the shares of smaller companies (or growth stocks) to keep the fund's performance numbers growing while equity markets are strong. Those are often the companies that fall the hardest when market sentiments change and investor enthusiasm vanishes. The illiquidity of these stocks can make it difficult for a fund that owns a large percentage of the company's shares to get out. As a result, the fund's net asset value can tumble, and this situation may be exacerbated by a heavy volume of redemption orders as fundholders attempt to sell.

Remember That It's Your Money

This is probably the most important rule to remember. No one can manage your assets better than you can. Yes, there are more knowledgeable people out there in terms of financial and market expertise, but their motivations will always be, to some extent, different from yours. Your goal should be to obtain the greatest amount of return with the least amount of risk. Their goal is to make money for themselves, and in this process, also make money for their clients. This is not meant to be a cynical statement, just an honest one. Most people employed in the investment industry want to make their clients money and do a good, honest job in trying to help the client achieve his or her goals. Ultimately, the more successful the investment professional is in helping his or her clients, the more money he or she will make. At the end of the day, however, the investment professional, whether successful results are achieved or not, does not have the same vested interest in a portfolio's closing value as the client does. For this reason, any individual who has money to invest should attempt to achieve a reasonable working knowledge of how the investment world works so as to best protect his or her assets.

With all of the time and effort that goes into making a living, everybody owes it to him or herself to earn as much as possible on what little money is left after taxes, bills, etc. Taking the time to learn about how to invest your money is essential. In this way you will increase your own control, and decrease the control that others have, over your financial future.

Consider the Benefits of Off-Shore Trusts and Corporations

Off-shore investing has become very popular in recent years. Books such as *Take Your Money and Run* by Alex Doulis have become best-sellers as Canadians look for ways to protect and preserve their wealth in the face of continuing tax hikes. If you decide that it is a good idea for you to keep some of your assets outside Canada, setting up an off-shore trust or corporation may be the best way to do it. My only advice in this area is that if you do take this kind of action, it is imperative that you seek the advice of a competent professional who has expertise in this field. This is necessary because these structures can sometimes be quite complex, and the tax laws and rules on off-shore investing are constantly changing. It is worth noting that once an off-shore corporation or trust is in place, it can hold almost any type of asset (including mutual funds or other investments).

While I'm neither endorsing nor condemning off-shore investing, when properly done it can be a legal way for Canadians to physically remove some or all of their wealth to another part of the world which has much more favourable tax rates. One of the fears that is indeed justified is that in the years to come, the government in Canada may be forced to implement currency controls that would deny citizens the ability to take their money out of, or invest it outside, the country. (Citizens of Great Britain experienced this situation several decades ago.) Currency controls have been used in the past when governments, close to insolvency, have needed all the money they could get their hands on from their citizens to begin the process of digging themselves out of the fiscal disaster at hand. While currency controls are often followed by higher tax rates and an inflating away of the country's debt, all citizens who reside in and have all of their assets within the country during this period suffer significant wealth loss. An off-shore trust or corporation could help to avoid this scenario as the money held within these structures could be invested outside of the individual's home currency and could be put into a wide variety of products. Today, one can open an off-shore account for as little $500 CAD in some cases. Individuals looking for more information on this topic should contact their lawyer or investment professional to obtain referrals to professionals who actively set up and administer off-shore investments.

Additional Information

For readers who would like more information on mutual funds and investing, I have a newsletter that tracks the many different mutual funds and investment products available in Canada and makes recommendations as to how best to implement the strategies mentioned in this book for the lowest cost. An analysis of current market conditions and changing legislation in the Canadian marketplace for investors will be provided. There will also be a hotline number which subscribers may call to receive additional information or ask questions on topics mentioned within the newsletter and this book. The annual subscription fee is $35.

For more information call Filipiuk Investment Corporation at (416) 369-4093 or write:

> Filipiuk Investment Corporation
> 13 Rue Gourgas #71
> 1205
> Geneva
> Switzerland

Notes:

1 Gordon Power, *The Globe and Mail*, April 19, 1997, p. B17.

Appendix A

The Stromberg Report and Beyond

More than five million Canadian adults, or about 26% of the population over 18 years of age, invest in mutual funds. This amazing statistic demonstrates the importance of the mutual fund industry and its increasing significance in the economy and lives of individual Canadians. The Canadian Securities Administrators (CSA), aware of the explosion in the creation and distribution of mutual fund units, or shares, were prompted to commission Glorianne Stromberg, a securities lawyer and one of the commissioners of the Ontario Securities Commission (OSC) to undertake a comprehensive review of the regulatory regime surrounding the industry. The chief reason for this review, according to her report, dated January 1995, was the need to have regulation keep pace with changes in the marketplace. The mutual fund industry itself, particularly the Investment Fund Institute of Canada (IFIC), the industry's member association, actively participated in Stromberg's study.

The stated goal of the review was better regulation, rather than more regulation, with emphasis on greater integrity in serving the needs of investors, whose interests must be paramount. Speaking of her report in October 1995, Stromberg said that the recommendations could be summed up as promoting two simple concepts: "fairness and integrity" and "information and knowledge".

The report proposes a new regulatory structure: a national commission, somewhat like the U.S. Securities and Exchange Commission, to eliminate, or at least reduce, the duplicate filing and registration requirements and the resulting cost in time and money. Unfortunately, the constitutional and regional concerns raised by the proposal are inhibiting the implementation of this cost-effective framework; there is now a growing feeling in the industry that the quest for a national securities regulator may be doomed.

The report also proposes the establishment of a "strong, independent, effective self-regulatory organization" (SRO), possibly modelled on the American National Association of Securities Dealers (NASD), which would operate on a national basis. Membership would be mandatory for everyone selling securities to the public. Representatives would be asked to focus on the development of common sales and business practices, and to produce a code of ethics for the investment industry. They would also address educational standards for industry participants and the issue of mandatory continuing education.

Stromberg's report considers the problems that exist with the present system of regulations. The industry faces a formidable compliance task already, with the Consolidated Ontario Securities Act and Regulations, 1995, running to 1285 pages, not including additional CSA policy and guidelines statements. Many sections are specific to mutual funds because of the recent rampant growth in the industry; and yet there are still regulatory gaps. Ms. Stromberg recommends the establishment of a Joint Regulatory Co-ordination Group, consisting of representatives of the Canadian banking, trust, loan, insurance, pension and securities regulators, and the self-regulatory organizations such as the Investment Dealers Association of Canada, the stock exchanges and consumer protection organizations like the Canadian Investor Protection Fund and the Canada Deposit Insurance Corporation. This Group would provide a co-ordinating mechanism to ensure that there are no regulatory gaps arising from:

"(i) deregulation of the financial services industry;

(ii) the entry of new participants into the marketplace; and

(iii) the multiplicity of regulators having jurisdiction over various aspects
of the business of the various participants in the industry."

A co-ordinating mechanism would also be sought to deal with international counterparts of this Group.

Ms. Stromberg's concern with "information and knowledge" relates both to industry participants and to the investing public. She correctly points out the need to improve the training, proficiency and conduct of sales personnel and to increase investor awareness and comprehension of investment issues. She recommends improvements in disclosure requirements so that information provided be "relevant," "timely" and "meaningful". The establishment of a basis for achieving comparability of performance information would be highly desirable.

Since its publication, the Stromberg report has produced considerable response from within the industry as well as without. The Ontario Securities Commission and the IFIC, answering the call to "fairness and integrity," have each drafted codes with respect to mutual fund sales practices. Not surprisingly, they differ in details on such matters as incentives, and other promotional items, familiar to readers of the financial press. That press has also recently underscored the report's concern with the integrity of those who work in the investment industry in any capacity, whose personal interests conflict or might conflict with the paramount interests of the investor and their fiduciary obligations to investors.

Examples of conflict, or potential conflict, abound, (most understandably), in the view of Stephen Erlichman. His paper, "*Fiduciary Obligations: Implications for Financial Institutions and Funds*," presented at the Osgoode Hall Law School of York University in October 1996, proposes a new analysis of the legal position of those engaged in the mutual fund industry. In a typical mutual fund structure, the trustee, manager and investment adviser and, in some cases, the registrar and transfer agent, are the same entity or entities, within the same corporate group, and thus naturally in a situation of potential conflict of interest. At the same time they owe a fiduciary obligation to their clients, an obligation which is of a much higher order of morality than that of the marketplace. It is Mr. Erlichman's thesis that the mutual fund industry is ripe for increased legal proceedings alleging breaches of fiduciary obligations (especially since contingency fees are now permitted in class actions in Ontario). Erlichman acknowledges that Ms. Stromberg's recommendations point in the right direction. She proposes that, as a condition of registration, investment fund managers be required to adopt a code of ethics and business conduct, setting out their policies with respect to personal investing (if personal investment by investment personnel is permitted). The media too is contributing to the cause of improvement by ferreting out information and publicising transgressions. *Caveat Emptor* seems to be making way for the enforcement of the principle of *Caveat Vendor*. The vendor is required to know the client and the suitability of the product for the client, and to follow through accordingly.

The media's role in this process of reform is important, and recently they have been feasting on accounts of behaviour within the industry, with descriptions ranging from "harmless transgressions" to "egregious misbehaviour" and "breaches of securities legislation and fiduciary duties". Piquancy is added when "stars" of the industry are involved, such as Frank Mersch, Veronika Hirsch, and firms of the stature of First Marathon Securities.

As a result, most mutual funds, and investment firms generally, have gone into committee on the codes that govern personal trading. The most prominent of such committees is probably that created by the Investment Dealers Association and Canada's four stock exchanges. The exchanges are no strangers to scandal, and urgency is added when firms like Bre-X Minerals Limited, Cartaway Resources Corp. and Timbuktu Gold Corp. financings hit the front page and stay there. The committee says it will conduct a policy review of "potential conflicts of interest which may occur from financing emerging businesses in Canada," and of rules governing investment personnel in their various roles as promoters, directors, officers and shareholders. Its report is expected to emphasize scrupulous disclosure and supervision. In another move toward reform, the IFIC and the IDA are discussing the subject of an Investment Funds Standards Board, as an interim step towards the single SRO recommended by the Stromberg report.

More progress has been made in the areas both of "fairness and integrity" and "information and knowledge". Until recently, for example, there was no way to assess the competence, conduct and ethics of financial planners who were aggressively promoting and selling mutual funds. This situation is now being remedied, however, following the creation of the Financial Planners Standards Council, which will award a "Certified Planner" designation based on licensing examinations. The Council hopes to become a self-regulating body, and has produced a code of ethics requiring planners to:

- Disclose any conflict of interest in writing,
- Recommend only those services needed by and appropriate to the client,
- Disclose sources and methods of compensation, and
- Provide advice only in areas in which the planner can show expertise

The Stromberg Report recommendations are a noble attempt to rationalize the regulation of the financial markets; however, history, geography, complexity and cost will ensure that the progress made will be relatively slow.

Appendix B

Labour-Sponsored Venture Funds

The number and popularity of venture capital funds has increased tremendously in recent years as the federal government and many of its provincial counterparts have offered some very lucrative tax credits to investors who purchase venture funds sponsored by some of Canada's labour and union movements.

What Are Venture Capital Funds?

Venture capital funds, by their very nature, are more risky than traditional mutual funds. The goal of venture capital funds is to find, and invest in, promising companies that are in their early stages of development. In most cases, these small companies are not listed on any exchanges and cannot obtain financing through any of the regular channels (i.e., no major bank, in most cases, would accept the risk level in lending to these companies, as they have very little, or no, collateral). Through investment in these companies, the venture capital funds take a high level of risk (taking an equity holding in the companies), but in return are assured a high level of return if the company eventually succeeds. In most cases the odds against success are great; however, if only a small percentage of the businesses succeed, the fund can do extremely well. The fundholders accept the risky nature of this type of investment and sacrifice the immediate liquidity that regular mutual fund investments enjoy.

Venture Funds and Tax Credits

In 1993, the federal government and most of its provincial counterparts (except Alberta and Newfoundland) agreed to provide tax credits to Canadian investors who purchased venture capital funds that were sponsored by labour or union movements. On a $5,000 initial investment, the purchaser would receive a one-time $1,000 federal and a $1,000 provincial tax credit. A great deal of marketing was done in showing how little money was at risk for the investor (in the top tax bracket) by purchasing the fund and using it as an RRSP contribution. (In Ontario, for instance, around $340 after-tax was at risk on a $5,000 investment in the top tax bracket.) The governments' motivation behind these credits was that these venture funds would invest their monies in Canadian enterprises (the funds had to operate under specific rules governing what qualified as a legitimate investment that would help in job creation and economic growth). Again, because of the attractive tax credits, the popularity of these funds took off, raising $3.6 billion by the end of 1996. Because of the attractive tax credits, many venture funds were set up that went around anxiously shopping for unions to sponsor them. As could be expected, many venture funds appeared to be set up for the sole purpose of receiving the tax credits, with little thought or no real mandate for investing.

Venture Fund Requirements

To receive the tax credits, the investor was required to stay invested in the fund for a minimum of five years, with some exceptions (i.e., retired individuals or those over 65 had to hold the fund for only two years, a statistic not unnoticed by many in the financial community). The venture funds could thus be assured that the money would not all be suddenly pulled out (remembering that most of these investments had very little or no liquidity at all). As a result of political pressure applied to the national and provincial governments to change these generous tax credits (the tax credits were seen as too generous and many funds were not investing quickly enough or in the desired areas), the rules were changed for the 1996 taxation year.

Currently, tax credits of 15%, both federally and provincially, are available on a maximum investment of $3,500 ($1,050 in total credits) and every investor must stay within the fund for a minimum of eight years. Sales in early 1997 were lower, as expected, given the changes brought in.

Anyone thinking of investing in venture capital funds should do some checking into the fund manager's past track record and the fund's investment mandate. These checks should be similar in nature to those done on regular closed- and open-end mutual funds. Most of the labour-sponsored venture funds have a sliding back-end load that begins at 6% for the first year and declines to 0% after seven. The funds are normally valued once a month, and it is at this time that purchases and redemptions are possible. The fund values appear in the mutual fund section of most newspapers and are easily followed.

One noticeable difference between most venture funds and regular mutual funds is the larger management ratios of the venture funds. Because of the labour-intensive nature of venture capital investing (a lot of work is necessary in seeking out and analyzing non-listed private companies) the annual management fees can often be in the 5-6% range. For some of the larger funds (i.e. Working Ventures with $827 million under administration as of June 30, 1997) the fees are often lower, given the economies of scale. It can therefore be prudent, in many cases, to look for a fund with a larger asset base so as to potentially reduce the overall costs on a percentage basis.

In conclusion, venture capital funds have the potential to achieve rates of return far superior to regular equity mutual funds, but they also present the possibility that the investor could lose everything. The investor should understand the risk inherent in this type of investment. The tax credits offered do give investors some downside protection, but they cannot prevent the investor from losing the after-tax money at risk, which in this case would be $2,450 of a $3,500 investment outside of an RRSP for 1997, or approximately $700 for purchases and contributions in an RRSP at the top tax bracket.

How To Reach the Fund Companies

Company	Telephone	Company	Telephone
20/20 Funds Inc.	800-268-8690	Investors Group	888-746-6344
ABC Funds	416-365-9696	John D. Hillery Investment Counsel Inc.	416-234-0848
Acadia Investment Funds Inc.	800-351-1345	Jones Howard Investment Mgnt. Inc.	800-361-1392
Admax Regent Group of Funds	800-667-2369	Laurentian Bank Investment Svcs Inc.	416-865-5832
AGF Management Limited	800-268-8583	Laurentian Funds Management Inc.	416-324-1617
AIC Limited	800-263-2144 Ont.	Leith Wheeler Management Ltd.	604-683-3391
All-Canadian Management Inc.	905-648-2025	London Life Insurance Co.	519-432-5281
Altamira Management Ltd.	800-263-2824 Ont.	Loring Ward Investment Counsel Ltd.	800-267-1730
AMI Private Capital	416-865-1985	Lutheran Life Insurance Society of Canada	800-563-6237
Associate Investors Ltd.	416-864-1120	M.K. Wong & Associates Ltd.	800-665-9360
Atlas Asset Management Inc.	800-463-2857	Mackenzie Financial Corporation	800-387-0615
Bank of Montreal Inv. Mgnt. Ltd	416-927-6000	Majendie Securities Ltd.	604-682-6446
Beutel Goodman Managed Funds	800-461-4551	Managed Investment Ltd.	800-287-5211
Bissett & Associates Investment	403-266-4664	Mandate Management Corporation	604-731-2899
BNP (Canada) Inc.	514-285-2920	Manulife Financial	416-229-4515
Bonham & Co. Inc.	800-408-2311	Manulife Securities International Ltd.	800-265-7401
BPI Mutual Funds	800-263-2427	Maritime Life Assurance Co.	902-453-4300
Burgeonvest Investment Counsel	905-528-6505	Mawer Investment Management	403-262-4673
C.I. Mutual Funds	800-563-5181	Maxxum Group of Funds	888-4-MAXXUM
Caldwell Securities Ltd.	416-862-7755	McDonald Financial Corporation	416-594-1979
Canada Life Assurance Co.	800-387-4447	McLean Budden Limited	416-862-9800
Canada Trust	800-668-8888	MD Management Ltd.	800-267-4022
Canadian Anaesthetists Mutual Accum	800-267-4713	Metropolitan Life Insurance Co.	800-267-9375
Capital Alliance Management Inc.	800-304-2330	Middlefield Resource Management Ltd.	416-362-0714
Capstone Consultants Ltd.	416-863-0005	MOF Management Ltd.	800-663-6370
Cassels Blaikie & Co. Ltd.	416-941-7500	Montreal Trust Co. of Canada	604-661-9535
Cdn. Dental Association	800-591-9401	Montrusco Associates Inc.	514-842-6464
Century DJ Fund	416-608-0727	Morrison Williams Investment Mgmt.	416-777-2922
Chou Associates Management Inc.	416-299-6749	Mutual Investco Inc.	519-888-FUND
CIBC Securities Inc.	800-268-5666	National Life of Canada	800-242-9753
Clarington Capital Management Inc.	888-860-9888	National Trust Co.	800-563-4683
Clean Environment Mutual Funds	800-461-4570	Navigator Fund Company Ltd.	204-942-7788
Co-operators Life Insurance Co.	800-667-8164	NN Life Insurance of Canada	416-391-2200
Colonia Life Insurance Company	800-463-9297	O'Donnell Investment Mgmt Corp.	800-292-5658
Confederation Life Insurance Co.	902-453-4300	OHA Investment Management Ltd.	800-268-9597
Corp. Financiers Du St-Laurent	514-288-7545	Ontario Teachers Group Inc.	800-263-9541
Cote 100 Inc.	800-454-2683 Que.	Optimum Placements Inc.	888-678-4686
CSA Management Ltd.	800-363-3463	Orbit World Fund	514-932-3000
Deacon Capital Corporation	416-350-3232	Pacific Capital Management Ltd.	800-662-5338
DGC Entertainment Ventures Corp.	800-EVC-1159	Peter Cundill & Associates Ltd.	800-663-0156
Dominion Equity Resource Fund Inc.	403-531-2657	Phillips, Hager & North Invest. Mgnt. Ltd.	800-661-6141
Dynamic Mutual Funds	800-268-8186	Primerica Life Insurance Co. of Canada	800-387-7876
Elliot & Page Ltd.	800-363-6647	Prosperity Capital Corporation	416-867-3863
Equitable Life Insurance Co. of Canada	800-387-0588	Puccetti Funds Management Inc.	905-649-5588
Ethical Funds Inc.	800-267-5019	Pursuit Financial Management Corp.	800-253-9619
Fidelity Investments Canada Ltd.	800-263-4077	Retrocom Growth Fund Inc.	888-743-5627
Fiducie Desjardins	800-361-2680	Royal Bank Investment Management Inc.	800-463-3863
First Marathon Securities Ltd.	800-661-FUND	Royal Life Canada	800-263-1747
First Ontario LSIF Ltd.	800-777-7506	Royal Trust	800-463-3863
Fonds des Professionels du Que.	800-363-6713	Sagit Management Ltd.	800-663-1003
Friedberg Commodity Management Inc.	800-461-2700	Sceptre Investment Counsel Ltd.	800-265-1888
GBC Asset Management Inc.	800-668-7383	Scotia Securites Inc.	800-268-9269
Gentrust Investment Counsellors	800-341-1419	Scudder Funds of Canada	800-850-3863
Global Strategy Financial Inc.	800-387-1229	Seaboard Life Insurance Company	800-363-2166
Globelnvest Funds Management Inc.	800-387-0784	Societe Financiere Azura Inc.	800-231-6539
Gordon Daly Grenadier Securities	800-268-9165	Spectrum United Mutual Funds Inc.	800-363-0414
Great-West Life Assurance Co.	800-665-0049	Sportfund Inc.	800-970-SPORT
G.T. Global Canada Inc.	800-588-5684	Standard Life	800-665-6237
Guardian Group of Funds	800-668-7327	Standard Life Mutual Funds Ltd.	800-665-6237
Guardian Timing Services Inc.	416-960-4890	Stone & Co. Limited	800-336-9528
Hongkong Bank Services Inc.	800-830-8888	Talvest Fund Management Inc.	800-268-8258
Howson Tattersall Investment Counsel	888-287-2966	Templeton International Inc.	800-387-0830
HRL Investment Funds	800-268-9622	The Bank of Bermuda Ltd.	441-299-5600
Imperial Life Assurance Co. (Can)	416-324-1617	The Empire Life Insurance Co.	613-548-1881
Industrial Alliance Life Ins. Co.	800-268-8882	The Enterprise Fund	800-563-3857
Integra Capital Management Corp.	416-367-0404	Top Fifty Financial Group	604-641-4511
		Toronto-Dominion Securities Inc.	800-268-8166
Integrated Growth Fund Inc.	800-420-5399	Tradex Management Inc.	800-567-FUND
InvesNat Mutual Funds	800-363-3511	Transamerica Life Insurance Co. of Cda.	416-290-2813

Company	Telephone	Company	Telephone
Triaz Growth Fund Inc.	800-407-0287	University Avenue Management Ltd.	800-465-1812
Trimark Investment Mgnt. Inc.	800-387-9845	Westbury Canadian Life Insurance Co.	800-263-9247
Trust General du Canada	800-280-3088	Working Opportunity Fund	604-688-9631
Trust Pret & Revenu	800-667-7643	Working Ventures Canadian Fund	800-268-8244

Index

Index

Index

Index

Index

Index

Index

Index

Index